# OBITS AND PIECES OF MY LIFE

## OF MY LIFE

### A Saga of Family, Friends and Basketball

## MICHAEL JON NAUGLE

outskirts
press

Outskirts Press, Inc.
http://www.outskirtspress.com

ISBN: 978-1-9772-5215-9

PRINTED IN THE UNITED STATES OF AMERICA

*Dedicated to*
*Hazel and Jack*

# Table of Contents

## Winter (But Early Winter...I Hope): 2007-present    181

## Adieu    197

# Introduction

I am a creature of habit. I'm 74 years old so I've had some time to develop habits, some good and some not so good, depending on who's noticing, but one of my most consistent habits is getting up in the morning (a good habit to be sure), walking out to the end of my driveway and retrieving *The Baltimore Sun* newspaper. Props to the newspaper deliverer, by the way, who rarely misses a morning delivery regardless of the weather. Fortunately for me, she too is a creature of habit.

I glance at the front page of the paper, the sports page and the weather on the back of the sports section as I saunter back up the macadam pathway to my home, but once I'm in the house and on my couch with a cup of black coffee in front of me, I open the paper to the obituary page. I don't have a morbid fascination with death; we've all got to go at some time, but I am always intrigued by stories of people's lives who have passed on. I have the utmost respect for obituary writers. I have no idea if this is a revered position to have as a newspaper journalist or if it's something the writer has resigned himself or herself to do because there are no openings for hard-core journalists who cover the life-altering stories, the stories that could propel them to Pulitzer-prize status. There should be a Pulitzer for obituaries. It fascinates me that a writer can sit down with a family member of a deceased loved one and in eight or ten paragraphs put together an all-encompassing life story of the dearly departed that makes you think, "Wow! This person had a really interesting life. I almost feel like I knew this person."

My goal in writing this autobiography was to write about my life as an eight- or ten-paragraph obituary. I have failed miserably. Maybe I can make it as a food critic.

*SPRING*

1947 to 1967

I've often wondered what my parents' lives were like growing up. Here I am, in the winter of my life (early winter I hope) as I begin this narrative, and I know very little if anything about my parents. They raised me. They provided for my needs. They seemed to like me and likewise, I them, but I don't think I ever really knew them, and I never took the opportunity to tell them how much I appreciated everything they did for me, which I sincerely regret. So, I'm putting together this little bit of personal history in order for my own kids and grandkids to gain a little historical perspective of my life. Now, it's not my intention to embellish accomplishments I may have achieved in my 74 years. My simple objective is to provide everyone with stories of the magical mystery tour of countless adventures in the life and times of Michael Jon Naugle. I'm fairly certain that my stories will not be the kind that would make one go, "Wow! That was a hell of a story there!" They're just remembrances of my life, some of which will have a story to them and some of which you'll read and think, "Why am I reading this?"

Let me begin with what I remember from my earliest years. This shouldn't take up too much of your time because I remember very little. I mean, there are brain cells that are refiring that I would've assumed would have died long ago from a lifetime of beer-infused family parties, weddings, funerals and related activities that always added a certain "je ne sais quoi" (I don't know what) to each and every occasion. I have been warned by my copy editor to refrain from using French language phrases, but I deemed it necessary here...Je ne sais pas pourquoi (I don't know why). Note: Many pages from now you'll read about my experiences in the Peace Corps in Niger, West Africa. I learned a little French there. What little I learned I'm proud to have retained. This book provides me with an opportunity to show-off. Now, back to my life's story.

What I do know for certain is that my father Jack, my mother Hazel, my brother Jack, Jr. (aka "Skip") and I moved to 38 Roessner Avenue in Halfway, Maryland, when I was one-year old. Halfway, incidentally, supposedly got its name because this community is located halfway between Hagerstown, Maryland, and Williamsport, Maryland, each being approximately three miles from Halfway—with Halfway being in the middle. It seemed to me as I grew up that both Hagerstown and Williamsport were a significant distance from Halfway. I remember taking a City Bus on Virginia Avenue (which is Route 11, a two-lane highway that begins in Montreal, Canada, snakes its way slightly to the southwest and finally ends up in New Orleans, Louisiana) by myself when I was eight years old to go to the YMCA in Hagerstown and thinking, "Whew! This will be quite an adventure. If this bus kept going, I'd be in Montreal." I'm fairly certain I didn't really think this but mindless thoughts like this will set the stage for what's to come. I feel compelled to warn you.

We moved to Halfway from East Avenue in Hagerstown, where my mother and my brother had lived in a duplex while my father was in Europe during World War II. I really don't remember too much from my infant years, hard as I try. I'm relatively sure that I was incredibly smart and had Gerber Baby bottle looks, but I can't be absolutely certain. I think that around three years old I began to notice that there were other people out there, and these were people who were imposing their will on me. I was no longer the most important person in the room. Life was never quite the same after this realization.

I guess my earliest memories are of the house in which I lived and the immediate surroundings, i.e., our backyard, which was probably a half-acre of land. It extended from the back porch to a grassy alley that divided Roessner Avenue and the back yards of houses on Lincoln Avenue. In between was a large apple tree. I remember this tree from an early age. It produced huge amounts of Transparent green apples. I should note here that Transparent apple trees were introduced to this country around 1870. No one really knows the country from which they came. There is no record of when someone planted a Transparent apple tree in our backyard, but it may have been the first Transparent apple tree in America. Also, this is not an apple that you can see through as the name suggests. It was much closer to translucent at best; closer to opaque really. It's a small, yellow, tart apple that will make your lips pucker when you try to eat one, but they make excellent pies. I remember my parents picking these green apples that to apple pie aficionados were at the top of the apple pyramid when it came to pies. Hazel also made apple sauce out of these things, but I don't recall the same accolades for the sauce being bandied about as for the pies. I believe Jack and Hazel sold some of the apples, but for the most part they were given away. During its peak production it was my job to gather the rotten apples in bushel baskets for disposal. The ground below the branches was so covered with rotten apples that walking under the tree was much akin to walking through a landmine field with squishy explosions occurring with every step.

When I was a little older, maybe ten or eleven, I used to find great joy in "twitching" these apples to other parts of our neighborhood. You could take an apple branch that was, say, a quarter of an inch thick and about two feet long, stick one these apples on it and fling it a good one hundred yards or more. It was amazing! At that age I figured that wherever they landed, no one would suspect where they came from, even though our giant apple tree was the only one of its kind on the block; maybe the only one left in America. Plus, they were transparent. Nobody could see them.

## Doggonit

Another feature of our yard was the wire-metal fence that marked the boundaries of our apple-infested half acre. Even from an early age I would climb the fence to get on the other side. No matter how big your yard might be, all a child wants to do is climb over the fence to get on the other side. I guess it's the "greener pastures" concept that makes us all think there must be something better there.

When I was five or six-years old, we had a "mutant" Boston Terrier named Pug that was white with black markings. Pug looked like a Boston Terrier on steroids. In my childhood I was probably bitten on several occasions by this lovable animal. Whenever this dog saw an opportunity to escape the confines of our yard, she would inevitably seek out small animals both wild and domestic to destroy. She had a reputation.

One of the peculiarities about Pug was that she could climb our fence and get out. She watched me and she learned how to do this. I've never seen another dog do that. Sadly, eventually Pug climbed over the fence one too many times. In her haste to devour a neighborhood cat, she was hit by a car and died an unfortunate but yet fitting death. Despite the proclivity of this dog to do dastardly things, I loved the animal, and when Jack broke the news of her passing to me, I was really upset. This was the first experience I had with death. Had there been an obituary writer for dogs, hers would've been short.

## K through 12, a Foundation Made of Bricks

When I was five, I began my formal public-school education at Lincoln Elementary School in Halfway. Based on its condition at that time, I'm guessing the school was built at the turn of the century. It was an ancient building that served all of the kids in the Halfway community from kindergarten through the 6th grade, and because of the large number of students, all of whom became known to modern America as "Boomers," a new school was needed. Boomers were the result of soldiers coming home from World War II and making up for lost time. Judging by the numbers of people who comprise the Boomer Generation, these veterans accomplished their goals.

The first year of my academic awakening was spent in the basement floor kindergarten room, across the hallway from the cafeteria. Mrs. Knapp was my teacher. I can imagine the cafeteria now because of the smell. It's funny how smells can trigger memories. The cafeteria had an unappealing smell, an odor that permeated every school cafeteria that I attended from K through 12. The fetid, vegetable-beef soup aroma was most certainly accentuated by the sauna-like steam heat that escaped unmercifully from the radiators in the basement of this ancient building. Even as a five-year-old I sensed that every day would be a challenge in this steaminess that was M.rs. Knapp's class. I remember the little plastic glasses of lukewarm and kind of thick orange juice that didn't quite taste like orange juice, and stale graham crackers for snacks. I remember that sweet, kind of minty white paste that was the paste of choice for art projects. I'm sure I must have tasted it from time-to-time to see if it was as good as it smelled. Finger-painting was another activity that I remember. Again, there was a smell associated with the finger-painting paint that bordered on nauseous. I don't remember wanting to taste finger paint after painting the outline of my hand. I also remember those fat crayons. I like crayons, even fat ones, but I remember Mrs. Knapp trying to pawn off those cheap waxy crayons on us; the kind that when you tried to color with them just slid over the paper with only a faint hint of color and no matter how hard you pressed, you were still left with the same discouraging results. Mrs. Knapp's son, Buddy, who was in later life one of my college roommates, was in her afternoon class. As I look back, I wonder if Mrs. Knapp saved the good crayons for her son's afternoon class? Conspiracy theories still abound.

## The First of Many

As was born in 1947, my guess is that I started the first grade in 1953. I'm not going to bore you even more with a year-by-year breakdown of my elementary school existence. I will highlight only the really important stuff, such as, I was always the second tallest kid in elementary school next to Richard Bowman. Even in the 5th and 6th grades someone would comment on my height but always with the caveat that Richard was a little taller. Had I been taller than Richard I think I would've been a better student. I would've been more confidant knowing that all of my fellow-students were shorter than me and I would not have had to deal with the stigma of only being the second-tallest. I had a lot to think about in those days.

My first-grade teacher at Lincoln Elementary School was Mrs. Wagner. I can't say that I was a good student in the beginning (or at the end for that matter) but I guess I began to learn the essentials that year. I was able to read that both Spot and Sally could run. This surprised me a little. I kind of knew that Spot could run but I thought Sally was a little slow of foot.

I guess when it gets right down to it, I remember things unrelated to the classroom as opposed to how I got to the classroom and the experiences I had along the way. I was almost six and a half years old when I started to school. I walked to school each day, and I recall that after the first week I walked by myself or with a friend. Lincoln Elementary School was only about two-and-a-half blocks from my house, but you had to cross Virginia Avenue to get there. A crossing guard always helped the children across, but as a six-year-old I felt both intimidated as well as liberated on this daily journey. In the back of my mind, I was always thinking that I could get run over by a car, but at the same time, I was crossing a busy highway every day on my own.

The other distraction from my actually being in school and learning something was Poole's Store, which after crossing Virginia Avenue was just down the street on Lincoln Avenue, across from the school. Poole's was like what Mall-of-America must have been to kids my age in Minnesota. They had everything! There were two display cases full of penny candy, there was a soda cooler which I vaguely remember being filled with ice and an ice-cream cooler with five-cent popsicles and fudgesicles. They had a post office in the rear of the building and there was one room for toys: everything from baseball cards, base-balls, kites, toy cars, dolls, just everything imaginable for someone my age. Candy bars and sodas were a nickel, and if you only had four cents to your name you could buy eight pieces of two-for-a-penny candies (I was never good at advanced math but I knew the basics). All of these things were housed in the downstairs of the Poole's home.

There were many days when I was supposed to stay on the school side of the street, but I would dart across and get candy at Poole's on the way home. While getting my first taste of formal education, I also developed a street-wise education which also had its benefits. For example, I knew that if I found an empty Coca Cola bottle on the side of the road on my way to school, I could take this bottle to Poole's and be rewarded with a $.02 refund for the return of the bottle and purchase 4 pieces of 2-for-a- penny candy. Black licorice was my drug of choice. Arithmetic was never my strong suit except when it came to the important things in life.

## Heading for Trouble

Miss Barton was my second-grade teacher. She was an older, diminu-tive lady and I vaguely remember that Miss Barton had a passion for diagramming sentences. This doesn't seem possible because I could barely write a sentence, much less diagram one. Once she started on prepositions, I was out of there. I mean, what kind of a preposition would you use to end a sentence with?

Another thing that I remember from that second-grade class was that it was the last year that my fellow-students and I sat at old wood-en desks, the kind you see in antique shops these days that most Boomers recognize but go unsold for the lack of knowing what to do with them. These were well-crafted and sturdy, wooden desks that had iron frames. The desk was connected to the chair back of the person in front of you, and there was a hole in the corner of the desk for an ink well; an ink well whose time had passed, I might add. Apparently though, these wooden desks would have saved me in the event of a nuclear bomb being dropped in the school yard adjacent to my classroom. I vaguely remember having drills where were told to get under our desks to shield if such a blast would occur. I often wondered if an atomic blast would really have been worse than having to sit and diagram sentences.

## Memories Are Made of This (Dean Martin Would've Been Proud)!

Grades three through six are kind of a blur. I do remember that I started the third grade at brand new Lincolnshire Elementary School which replaced the old Lincoln Elementary School. I remember bits and pieces of each of these grades. I remember learning cursive writing using those metal quilled pens that we'd used to dip the pen in a small jar of ink and then attempt to write letters of the alphabet on lined white paper. The end result inevitably led to a line of blotched letters, one indistinguishable from the other. Errant drops of ink on my khaki pants were another unforeseen result of this endeavor. I wore permanently in ink-blotched pants during my entire third grade year. I did learn how to write in cursive but the experience dampened my enthusiasm (and my pants) for using this skill in actual practice. Printing words remained my writing method of choice from then on up to the present.

Elementary school was easy for me, very little pressure. Other than the curveball that Miss Barton tried to throw me, I wasn't subjected to symbols and equations, just your basic math. I believe Mrs. Reams, my fourth-grade teacher, attempted to throw me off balance when she tried unsuccessfully to teach the metric system and the importance of knowing this because that would be our future method of measurement. We all know how that turned out.

My sixth-grade music teacher emphasized the importance of reading music, but differentiating between a quarter note and a half note left me more than half confused. I took up the drums but I had to rely on rote memory and natural rhythm. My natural rhythm wasn't too bad but my rote memory made for some challenging moments.

## Time Skates By

My world from ages five to eight revolved around the immediate half-block area in which I lived. To my right as I faced out onto Roessner Avenue lived Joyce Conrad, five years my senior. Close to the Naugle house lived George Orange, a friend through high school, and Margie Cushion, who I found out obtained a Phd. in French and I was envious of her accomplishment. Immediately across the street lived Billy Fridinger, who was a few years younger and directly to the left of the Fridinger's lived Jimmy Scott. All these neighborhood kids (except Joyce) were more or less the same age as me and these were the kids that I generally played with during this time.

Let me start with Joyce Conrad. As mentioned, Joyce was about five years older than me. Joyce taught me to ride a bike when I was six. She took me to my first movie at the old Henry's Theater in Hagerstown to see "Westward Ho the Wagons" when I was seven or eight. Joyce was an important part of my life at that time as well as a family friend for many years after. The other memory I have of Joyce, aka "Butch," is that hers was the first family I knew who owned a television set.

At that time, television was kind of a miracle. I mean, there were the movies of course but to bring movies and television shows into your home, that was pretty magical. This was about 1952 or '53, and during different days of the week I remember going next door to Joyce's family's house to watch Buffalo Bob introduce us to Howdy Doody, the Lone Ranger and Tonto, Gene Autry, Roy Rogers and Dale Evans; all of these incredible kids' shows that totally mesmerized me at that time of my life. When I hear the William Tell Overture, my introduction to classical music, I always think back to those days.

I loved cowboy and Indian movies back then. I recognize that in the 21st century we are more sensitive to terms that are degrading to some people, like the term "Indian," but "cowboys and Native Americans or indigenous people" would not have rolled off our tongues as easily.

When we finally able to afford a television in our house, my favorite shows were still shoot 'em up Westerns, but then one rainy Saturday afternoon in 1955 my passion for Westerns was forever changed. There were still only three channels you could watch then, CBS, NBC and ABC, and on this one particular gray and damp Saturday afternoon, I was physically turning the channel knob in search of a western movie and I came upon this movie called "Oklahoma." Now, my initial reaction was "Oh yea!" I'd settle back on the family couch preparing myself for an action-packed movie. It started out with potential but then something very strange happened. The cowboys started singing and dancing. Now, Roy Rogers and Dale Evans would sometimes end their show with a song, and Gene Autry would strum a cowboy song, but they never interfered with the action of the story. In Oklahoma, everything these cowboys and cowgirls did in this new movie was done in song. It made no sense to me. My disdain for musicals began on that wintry afternoon in 1955. Maybe if I had been fore-warned I would not have been so confused, and could have switched channels and watched the Ted Mack Amateur Hour.

In the same vein there was the 1953 movie, Peter Pan. I guess I was younger when this movie came out on television and a little more gullible but even then, at six-years old, I could not understand why Peter was a girl. Who was responsible for such a decision? I would have been okay with "Petra" Pan. No one could seem to explain why these changes took place. Television was embedded in my youth and I loved it but I was sensing even then, that there were people behind the scenes who were messing with my psyche. I could devote a whole book on "The Sound of Music" but I'll leave well enough alone except to say that when Maria made those kids play clothes made out of drapes, I thought my head would explode!

## On the Street Where You Live
## (Vic Damone and Jimmy Scott)

Jimmy Scott lived across the street from me. Jimmy and I were close friends in elementary school. I remember that we converted an old chicken coop in his backyard to a "club." We called it the "Eagle's Club." I think we were the only members, but it was kind of neat having this secret hideaway that only we knew about. Jimmy and I would go to the YMCA in Hagerstown when we were about nine or ten. Jimmy was an excellent swimmer and was on the "Y" team. We sort of went our separate ways in junior high school; I'd see him and say hi, but that was about it. In the ninth grade Jimmy was diagnosed with leukemia, and he died during his freshman year at South Hagerstown High School. I regret not having been a better friend to him during those later years. His birthday is January 18th and I remember him every year on his birthday. People should not die young. I still have the "Open" sign we had from the "Eagle's Club," on a converted dry sink we use as a bar.

All of my evening outdoor play was confined to the sidewalks and street in front of my house. Tag, hide and seek, touch football in the street, shooting baskets in Jimmy Scott's driveway and roller skating on the sidewalks were among the many recreational activities in which we indulged. Roller skating in particular had its many ups and downs (so to speak). We used those metal skates with leather straps that you connected to your shoes with clamps that you tightened between your shoe tops and the leather soles. Leather shoes were essential. Sneakers just didn't cut it. The clamps were tightened with a metal skate key. Occasionally these days a skate key will pop upon Facebook, and someone will post, "Does anyone remember what this is?

There are random pieces of information that I remember, trivial things that have little value but come to mind frequently for no apparent reason. Here's an example: I was skating one day on the sidewalk when I was seven or eight years old, and a classmate of mine, Donna, who lived in the neighborhood and who shared a passion for roller-skating stopped by. Donna, who I believe in later life became a social worker and hospital administrator or something, skated down the street from her house to the paved sidewalks on my street. The usual childhood banter ensued as we skated as fast as we could on the smoothest sections of the sidewalk.

At some point when there was an interlude because our skates became unhinged from our shoes, we'd start talking about our lives. Donna revealed to me that she hated her shoes. These were also her everyday school shoes. They were brown lace-up Buster Browns (no sign of Tige inside; something that Boomers would be looking for). I think that in the early 50's correctional shoes were all the rage. I can only assume that our parents lived through terrible times during the Great Depression where shoes were not only hard to come by, but also whatever shoes one was able to come by were the shoes one would wear, regardless of the size, thus causing foot problems. There was something to this shoe situation that intrigued me.

Donna was angry at her parents for forcing her to wear these un-girly-type shoes to school. These were boys' shoes. I actually felt sorry for her. Instinctively I sensed the indignity of it all. I wondered what it would be like if I had to wear Mary Janes to school. We started talking about other things we hated, and she blurted out that she absolutely hated canned peaches. I mean, this was a deep conversation. This dialogue has stuck with me all these years. I think of Donna every time I open a can of peaches; the shoes, not so much, but I still remember the conversation. I messaged Donna recently on Facebook and asked her if she remembered hating canned peaches. She messaged me back and said she still hates canned peaches. There are some things that time simply can't heal.

## The Wonder Years

As I got a little older, maybe eight or nine, I began to expand my recreational territory to include a wider range of space and friends in the neighborhood. For the most part, the names of many of this new cast of characters escape me, but John Trantules, Bobby Weaver, Larry Hayes, Robby Rice, "Bug" Shriver, Jimmy Mace, Tony Cianelli, Mike Leiter, Chip Dorsey, Chuck Beachley and others were the foundation of an all-encompassing sports and related recreation activities group. As you will later read in this book, in the late 1970's I received a Master's degree in Urban Recreation from the University of Baltimore. The foundation for this degree was based on these early childhood recreation experiences. Some kids dream of being a star athlete, a doctor, a lawyer or maybe an architect. I dreamed from an early age of becoming a recreator. Sometimes dreams indeed come true.

In the summer months, almost every day revolved around pick-up baseball games at the "tennis court." At the end of Roessner Avenue where it meets Virginia Avenue, there was a long-forgotten tennis court with a typical high metal fence that was on the property of the Odenhalls. The Odenhalls were, as far as we knew, the richest people in Halfway. Whether that was the case or not, the perception by our member group was that they were. In our eyes their home was a mansion and it had an in-ground swimming pool that was simply unheard of in those times. Included also on the Odenall's property was what had been its heyday a private clay tennis court. The tennis standards on the old court were still intact but its use as an actual tennis court no longer existed. Someone, maybe of my brother, Skip's era, saw the potential for a baseball field in this neglected space. No one seemed to object and it became for many summers a baseball field for elementary-age kids in the community.

My friends and I from those days began playing baseball on this re-converted field in the 50's. It had become a weed-infested court with two tennis standards with no nets. The tennis standards (the two poles that originally held the net) became first base and third base, respectively. Second base and home plate could be either a piece of cardboard, someone's jacket, hat or an unused baseball glove, depending on the importance of the game or the availability of these makeshift bases. I guess hundreds of games were played there in the 50's but the biggest feature of the (now baseball) field was the tall fence and hedge that engulfed the fence at the Virginia Avenue end. This was Halfway's equivalent of the Green Monster in Fenway Park in Boston. The only official record of how many home runs were hit there was in the minds of the players who hit them, and if someone said that he had hit 14 home runs that particular season, it was believed. It was an honor system that was honored. There were "special" home runs that were engraved in the Hall-of-Fame minds of all the players. These were the home runs that majestically rose over the faux Green Monster and managed to break a car window of an unsuspecting driver on his to Montreal or the "The Big Easy." This generally ended whatever game was being played that afternoon, as the players scattered in all directions on their bicycles. I remember my brother Skip (six years older than me) pulling up in his car one afternoon and saying, "Hit it over the fence," and I did. That was probably the most memorable round-tripper that I had there. The most I ever hit in a season was 7…but who's counting?

## The Spectacle of Things

I'd like to interject here that I started wearing glasses in the first grade. This doesn't seem to go with the flow of things, but I just thought of it while trying to think of ways to keep the flow going. Glasses certainly help with the clarity of things, but throughout my childhood they were a source of consternation. I always thought of myself as "athletically inclined." I felt I could have been much better at sports, but the fear of breaking my glasses, and the wrath of my mother when I told her that I broke my glasses but it wasn't my fault and the wait that ensued in getting a new pair (Remember wearing an old pair while waiting? It felt like seeing through a pair of binoculars that you couldn't quite bring into focus.) hindered my ability to fully participate in sports to the best of my ability. Subconsciously I was always afraid of getting hit by a baseball or being flattened in a sandlot football game— things like that. My fear was not getting hurt. My fear was breaking my glasses. As a result, even as I got older, I tended to lack the fearlessness that would've taken me to a higher performance level. My hope in writing this is to garner some sympathy from the reader as well as explain why I always seemed to average 4.0 points a game in basketball regardless of the level in which I played.

## Keep Your Head above the Water

The other summer activity which I loved was swimming, which didn't require glasses, although goggles were a welcome addition. Once a week during the summers in my grade-school years, Hazel would take me to the Municipal Swimming Pool on Frederick Street in Hagerstown. I loved that pool. When you arrived in the parking you could smell the chlorine. That, mixed with the intense heat of the day is a memory I sense every time I swim in an outdoor pool in the summer or an indoor pool in the winter. Our sense of smell is a wonderous thing. Supposedly, it brings back more memories than any of our other senses.

The Hagerstown Municipal Pool was an oasis of aquatic activity in those days. I kind of remember the whole experience from arriving in anticipation of an exciting day in the water to leaving exhausted but wishing you didn't have to wait another week to come back. I remember the little details like paying a quarter at the entrance of the pool and entering a crowded locker room to change clothes. Admittedly, the locker room was somewhat intimidating. You were assigned a locker by the "Locker Boy." His job was to keep everything in order, and God forbid that you should challenge his authority or station in life. Upon assignment you would receive an elastic band with your locker number on it, and you were required to wear this band around your ankle at all times while in the pool. Before entering the pool area, you were forced to stand in a cold shower at the door and you had to walk through a flat, rubber vat of chlorine, the purpose of which I assume was to kill any foreign organisms known to man at that time. The Locker Boy and his cronies always made sure that this tortuous procedure was followed as directed or you could not enter the pool.

Once in the pool, life was good. I just remember spending hours there as a little kid, always testing fate by trying to slip into the 4' level beyond the rope divider just to be able to say to my friends that I swam in the deep end.

My other favorite swim destination when I was young was Cowans Gap State Park just north of Fort Loudon in Pennsylvania. The Park, which includes a 42-acre lake, was constructed during the Great Depression by Franklin Roosevelt's Civilian Conservation Corps. From the time I was 5 or 6-years-old through my high school years, I can remember my parents taking me on day trips during the summer to Cowans Gap and in later years spending week-long vacations there at rented homes every summer. Ultimately, they purchased a cabin where they spent many weekends during their later life. I loved those summer vacations. I have great memories of being on the beach and swimming there every day. Jack had restored an 18' Old Town Canoe from a skeletal frame and created a fiber glass shell for the boat that formerly was a canvas-covered boat. That may have been the heaviest Old Town canoe in history at its completion but it was glorious, and I canoed every inch of the lake at Cowan's Gap over the years in that boat. The pine trees left an indelible memory in my mind much like the chlorine at the Municipal Swimming Pool in Hagerstown. To this day, if I take a week-end hike in the nearby Catoctin Mountains or any pine-forested park, even in winter, the pine smell reminds of those summers over a half-century ago.

My last related swimming story is not quite as memorable as the previous two stories but it is funnier. Every spring, beginning when I was maybe ten or eleven years old, usually in the middle of March, a bunch of us thrill seekers would get on our bikes and ride about a mile or so towards Williamsport to Alvin Massey's family farm. They had two ponds on the farm: one had extremely cold water that the cows would swim in, and the other was warmer and may have been where the cows had previously swum. We chose the warm pond regardless of who may have swum there. The objective was to be the first outdoor swimmers of the new year. (As for the cows, I'm pretty sure they swam year-round, so bragging rights would not seem to have been their objective, and I'm relatively sure they didn't have to tiptoe into a vat of chlorine solution before entering their pond.) The cows appeared to be quite happy and became known amongst us as the *Les Vaches qui rient* or "Laughing Cows".

Actually, I just threw this in. When Cass (my wife who will appear much later in this book) and I were in the Peace Corps over a quarter of century after we swam with the cows, the only "safe" cheese we could purchase in the town in which we lived in Niger was "La Vache qui rient". I do remember this cheese from when I was young and I remember it as something that I could tolerate but didn't care for. Of course, in America it was "Laughing Cow" cheese but I never made this connection until we were in the Peace Corps many years later. Combining this cheese along another favorite international food product, Vienna sausages and well, you have a veritable smorgasbord of haute cuisine.

## Fall Ball

The end of summer has always brought a sense of sadness to me. The freedom of summer was always exhilarating. I could be myself. I could try new things; sometimes with great success and sometimes with failure but always without judgement. The start of the Fall meant the start of another school year. I can't say I was never excited about it but I knew there would be regimentation, academic expectations along with academic failures that I'd feel guilty about. None-the-less, I prepared myself to cope with whatever came my way. If nothing else, I was resilient and there were still afterschool and weekend activities to quell my school-room anxieties.

The fall months were dedicated to football in some secretly-discovered sandlot, sometimes a school yard and sometimes somebody's backyard, but the games were fun and, despite classifying them as "tackle" games, I don't remember anyone suffering any serious injuries during those years. There were no recorded stats, but all of us knew and would recount for days a good play or who scored the winning touchdown, and the games were discussed in the ensuing days like people do in an office at the water cooler.

I was eight or nine when I began to develop an interest in basketball. My brother would watch games on television on a Saturday afternoon. I was inclined to want to watch a Western movie, but my brother was six years older and inclined to watch what he wanted to watch. My first basketball games were conducted on somebody's driveway with a hoop connected to a garage and generally not connected particularly well. There were a lot of bent hoops sans nets. The ten-foot measurement also was very arbitrary on these less-than-smooth macadam courts.

Regardless of the differing conditions of the basketball standards, I felt an attraction to the game. It didn't consume me. I never dribbled a basketball to school or spent hours lofting errant shots from grass spots adjacent to a paved driveway. My father (Jack) actually constructed a basketball standard in our backyard, and it was a really good piece of construction. It was another one of those things that I never appropriately thanked Jack for. There was no paved area from which to shoot, but the grass court eventually turned into a hardened dirt surface and became an acceptable playing surface for my purposes.

## Young Men's Christian Association

My game began to improve exponentially (and "exponentially" is a relative term) when I started going to the YMCA in Hagerstown. The Hagerstown YMCA was this massive brick building that sat pretty much at the top of the hill on North Potomac Street. It was a classic, universal-in-design YMCA and was a typical "Y" of that time. I should add this historical footnote before moving on. The Young Men's Christian Association was founded in the mid-1800's on the principle of "muscular Christianity." I was never muscular, and my Christianity began to wane early on when subjected to Sunday sermons at the Church of the Holy Trinity in Halfway that challenged my attention deficit issues to the max. If there truly was a merciful God, He/She would have eliminated sermons and found another way to communicate to the masses. Invariably, like many times in life when I let my guard down and prayed to God, my prayers were never answered and there were very few short sermons.

Back now to the description of the Y that I loved in my youth. In the basement of the building there were pool tables (real tables with leather pockets), a large crafts area that included an actual working shop where you could sand and grind things like plastic rings (as in rings for your fingers) and pre-made sculpted plaster of Paris pieces including flowers, dogs, people and other such random items. You would pay anywhere from ten cents to a quarter to have the privilege of trying to turn your selected craft into a work of art, and generally you had about a half an hour to do so. In my case the time frame was dependent on the level of attention deficit I was experiencing on that particular day. I don't ever remember completing a craft, but nonetheless I loved the process.

Also on the lower level was a large general-purpose room that served as a lunchroom and movie theater on Saturdays. I remember my mother packing me a brown bag lunch and giving me money to buy a drink from the upstairs main lobby. Once this purchase had been made I returned to the lunch/movie room, and we'd watch "The Three Stooges" and related short comic adventures while eating our lunches. Now this may seem like a trivial inclusion here, but it's another one of those random memories that made an impact on me. I enjoyed those times.

At the concession counter in the main lobby, they sold a variety of snacks, chips, pretzels, candy bars, etc., but they had a soda cooler and freezer that held my very favorite items. The first was Frosty Root Beers. Now, you sometimes still see Frosties in supermarkets or maybe in Cracker Barrel's specialty aisles, but they're nothing like those Frosties were. Those Frosties were sold in squat, really substantial glass bottles, and I think they may have been 12-oz. bottles which was unusual for that time. Cokes for example, came in 6 ½ ounce bottles. The Y's cooler kept them at near freezing. The root beer had a hint of vanilla and it was a smooth carbonated drink, as opposed to a gaseous carbonation that one might get from a Coke (which I also loved but not at the Y). It was just the best drink. It was a drink that you looked forward to and savored every last drop. If you still had money left over from your Frosty, the other item was Fudge O's. These were short fat fudge bars (substantial might be a better description), and the freezer at the Y kept them near rock-like. It took you ten minutes to get through one of them because if you weren't careful your lips would get stuck on them as you ate them. These items were my all-time favorites.

The lower level of the Y also housed the swimming pool. I mentioned earlier that my childhood friend Jimmy Scott was an outstanding swimmer and member of the swim team at the Y. I enjoyed swimming but had a problem with how they conducted their "free" swims. Boys weren't allowed to wear bathing suits. We had to swim naked if we wanted to enjoy a swim as part of our Saturday experience. Swimming naked in front of adult male lifeguards as well as my peers was such a personal concern for me that after I was ten or eleven years-old I never swam at the YMCA again. The only explanation given at the time was that lint or material from your swim shorts would clog the pool filter. That made me even more suspicious. I was relatively sure that my swim trunks contained no lint. When the Y team swam against other Y's, the swimmers wore swim suits. I guess those plaid, boxer-type swim suits that we used to wear must've somehow generated huge amounts of lint. It's an unsolved mystery of to this day.

Although it was the Young Men's Christian Association, there were girls who attended the Y and I assume had some sort of organized "girl" activities, but I have no idea to this day what those activities may have been. Girls must have had a secret entrance because it was extremely rare that I even saw a girl there but...they were there... somewhere. Even at ten or eleven the boys knew something was going on. The one particular thing that we all wanted to know was, do the girls swim naked? That would've been okay. When we suspected they were in the pool (which they most assuredly entered through a secret portal), we would sneak up to what we were sure was an entrance that none of us had ever used and peek through cracks to see if we could catch a glimpse of these naked girls swimming in the pool in which only naked boys could swim. We were never successful, but when our early pubescent hormones kicked in, we would still make the effort. We were a determined lot.

From the lower floor men's locker room from which you could enter the pool, there was a long set of about thirty wooden steps that led up to the second-floor gym. I couldn't wait to get to the top step, open the door and walk into the arena of my youth. The smell added to the fetid ambiance. It was a stale sweatiness that had permeated into the wood over generations from perspiring basketball players, volleyball players, runners, weightlifters, etc., who exuded their manly smells in their respective sports. You felt kind of grounded in the atmosphere. This is where you wanted to be (as long as you could wear shorts). There was a certain manliness about the place. It was a good feeling.

The Y gym was a replica of most Y gyms that had been constructed in the 20's. There was of course the basketball court that could interchangeably be used for other team sports. There were two adjacent weight rooms to the side of the gym and this incredible overhead wooden oval running track that circled above the gym. You also had to take a large flight of stairs to get up to the track. I believe the track was an eighth of a mile long, and it was "banked" at each curve. I was never a runner, but nonetheless I would go up there periodically and run as hard as I could, especially on the curves, and marvel how I had to adjust my stride while rounding the curves. Over the years, especially during the winter months, there were many sanctioned indoor-track meets on this track. I never could understand the fascination with just running, but I was intrigued by those who did and always wondered why they would spend their time doing that when they could come back down the steps and shoot hoops.

When you shot baskets at the Y, you had to allow for the running track; its curves above your head would protrude out over the gym's four corners. Your shot had to be adjusted to compensate for this overhang. Shooting a basketball with an arc could not be done in any corner of the gym. I think that the inability to raise my shot from the corners of the Y gym as an aspiring twelve-year-old professional basketball player may have been a major contributor in my not being able to fulfill my ultimate dream of playing for the Boston Celtics. I mean, seriously, what else could it have been?

I loved the YMCA, but I would like to note something that will appear in a little more detail in future chapters. When I was ten or eleven years-old I had just mounted the steps from the locker room and entered the gym and was about to begin another day of athletic endeavors when I noticed another kid standing there nervously looking at what this place held in store for him. This new and unexpected member was Black. It never occurred to me that there were no Black kids at the Y, and it wasn't until years after that I understood the racial inequities of those times. Many of the same inequities most certainly exist in the 21$^{st}$ century, but laws at a minimum protect minorities from "overt" racist actions. But as to the young guy who mysteriously showed up at the gym, I vaguely remember him just getting involved in whatever activity my friends and I were about to do. We just continued doing what we were doing and that was that. My sense is that there were no issues, which of course there shouldn't have been, and after that I believe that more Black kids assimilated into Y programs.

I recently asked Vernon Stoner, a former Black acquaintance and high school basketball team member, about those times. I asked where he and his friends went for recreation activities. His answers didn't surprise me and certainly reinforced my suspicions. Black kids, boys in particular, did not have lot of options. Vernon said that he and his friends would go to the Optimist Boys Club, which was right behind the YMCA. I remember walking down the street that ran along the side of the Y and wandering into the Boys Club out of curiosity. At the time I never considered that this was the only place for kids of color to go. Vernon also said that they'd play basketball and other sports in Wheaton Park, which I guess was, by social design, a park for Black people who lived in the Jonathon Street corridor, the area where at that time probably 99 percent of the African-American population of Hagerstown lived. Vernon also mentioned that his parents made him as well as his siblings attend church three times a week. I'm sure the church played a significant role in that community. It was probably the one unifying place where people could congregate in safety and enjoy one another's company in a social setting. I was oblivious at that time to racial issues. It took years for me to understand how difficult life must have been in Hagerstown if you were Black.

## Winter Wonderland

My outdoor winter activities included a smattering of the aforementioned sandlot football and basketball games, but there were also two other winter recreational pursuits. Climate change was not on the minds of our recreation cohort 65 years ago. Cold was not an issue, and a welcome change to the dreariness of January occurred if school was cancelled because of snow. No matter what, there was this giddy sense of joy that came over me, knowing that I didn't have to go to school. My second reaction was, "Oh man! Sledding!" The third thing that came to mind was that Hazel (my mother) would shame me into going out and shoveling neighbors' sidewalks for money. Admittedly, I did enjoy having this windfall of extra money to spend but my thoughts remained with sledding.

The first big snow collectively drew the entire neighborhood to Buzzard's Hill. Buzzard's Hill was at the end of Gay Street in Halfway. It intersected with Lincoln Avenue. At the intersection you would take your wooden sled with the well-worn rope from previous winters, and in some cases previous owners, and begin the trek to the top of the hill. In reality this hill from top to bottom was about 100 feet, but to us, it was our Mont Blanc. We would spend an entire day slogging up the hill and then propel our sleds down the hill at what we thought were supersonic speeds. When I came home in the late afternoon I would literally be suffering from frostbite. I remember trying to get those damn rubber boots off. The metal snaps were frozen, your fingers were frozen, and your feet were frozen. Once you somehow managed to pry off your boots, you'd start experiencing tingly sensations in your fingers and toes. You would stand by the register (metal grate) in the hallway with the heat coming up from the coal-fired furnace in the basement, and you would silently pray that the prickly pain you were coping with in your hands and toes would soon subside; and fortunately, after a time it did. Amputation was not an option on that particular day.

The other childhood memory I have of winters is ice skating on the Conococheague Creek at Kemp's Mill, just north of Williamsport, Maryland. For the sake of the uninformed, the mighty Conococheague runs about eighty miles from Pennsylvania through Maryland and then empties into the Potomac River in Williamsport. Winters in those times were cold—cold enough to freeze the Conococheague. At some point during winter, someone (no one ever knew who) determined that the ice on the creek was at least a foot thick, and that was the determining factor in skating on it. My father took me. There would always be a surprising number of skaters testing the quality of the ice. You could skate all the way from Kemp's Mill to the Route 40 Bridge two or three miles north. From time to time, you would hear the ice crack. It was eerie because it was more than just a loud crack; there was a whistle-like sound that resonated around you. Sometimes you thought that at any second the ice would implode and you'd be struggling to swim to shore while wearing a heavy coat and ice skates.

I could only skate with figure skates. To this day I cannot skate with hockey skates. I was a good skater, but with figure skates only. (That's not so bad. I had an uncle in Chambersburg, Pennsylvania, my mother's only brother, who supposedly could only skate backwards. The type of skates was not an issue with him. For some reason he could not skate forward. I'm told that he was a hell of a skater—but only backwards.)

We always played games of hockey. None of us had hockey sticks or pucks. I don't think helmets would've been a consideration regardless of how well we may have been outfitted to play. (Did you know that helmets in professional ice hockey were not required until 1974?) We searched for the best tree branch available on the sides of the creek, hopefully one with a 90-degree angle at the end, and we used beer cans, soda cans or empty cans of beans for pucks, whatever was available in the brush and dead branches along the shore. Games were highly competitive, and on those particular days we all aspired to be professional hockey players. I think if I had had the ability to do a triple-axle prior to a slap shot and if my uncle could quickly skate backwards to keep the opposition from scoring, we could have changed the game of hockey forever.

Everything that I've written about to this point has been about the fun parts of growing up in Halfway. Running around the neighborhood and reveling in the freedom of being a kid unencumbered by parental supervision was a thrill.

## Yippee!

When I was about eleven years old I started playing competitive sports. I played Junior League Basketball for the Rotary Club and for Dixon-Troxell American Legion. The games were played at the old North Potomac Junior High School on North Potomac Street in Hagerstown. I loved the idea of being on a team and I could not wait to get to the weeknight games. The problem was, I couldn't play in games. I would get into games, but I always froze. I got the "yips." I always had a fear of failure, and as a result I failed. I don't know where this lack of confidence originated, but I had to work all my life to overcome or compensate for this flaw. Humor was how I compensated, but occasionally something would occur that gave me enough confidence to spur me on. I was always a good recreational athlete but when I put on a uniform, games were a struggle.

When I was twelve years-old I played Little League Baseball for the first time. My brother had always played competitive sports. He was 6 years older than me. My parents, who worked very hard, were involved in his sports to my detriment. They did not take summer vacations, mainly because my brother would have competitive baseball games that necessitated transporting him to and from games and practices. When my time rolled around, my parents wanted to have summer weekends and vacations for themselves (and me as well, of course), and they certainly deserved to do this. At any rate, I wasn't allowed to go out for baseball until I was twelve, the last year I would be eligible.

I loved baseball and as previously noted I played a lot of sandlot baseball, but I wasn't particularly good, and the "yips" played a part in my development or lack thereof as well. I played for Culler's Esso in the Halfway Little League. I played some in every game, but I couldn't hit, mainly because I was afraid to get hit. As a result, I didn't get a lot of hits; in fact, I had two hits the entire season, one a double (which both surprised and thrilled me and one that Chip Dorsey said was a "lucky hit."), and the other a grand slam home run in the very last game of the season. I guess I shouldn't have to point this out, but a grand slam is a homer hit with the bases loaded, which means that my home run was responsible for four runs. I think my father may have been at that game. I was beside myself—I mean, that made up for a very frustrating season. Our team lost 7 to 4, but that didn't matter. The next day in the Hagerstown *Daily Mail* Sports Section there was a feature on all of the Little League Games in the area, and under the Halfway Little League they wrote (and I'm paraphrasing): "Culler's Esso lost the game, but Mike Naugle hit a towering grand slam home run, and even though his team lost 7 to 4 he could not have cared less. It was the greatest home run in his career—and the only one." Chip Dorsey told me after the game that if he would've been playing in that game, he would've caught it.

I have now pretty much encapsulated my youth up to the age of twelve, not like a really good obituary would in six or eight paragraphs, but I never claimed to be a good obituary writer.

## A Somewhat Lengthy Family History with an Appreciation Component

I would like to include a chapter on the significance of my parents during my first twelve years and beyond. My guess is that it is only natural to take your parents for granted. Some people might disagree with this, but how many of you thought about your parents buying you something you really wanted or really supporting you in some cause that you were passionate about and afterwards taking the time to thank them? If I could fast-forward thirty years, both my wife Cass and I did everything we could to provide our kids with the best opportunities possible to try to ensure that they would have a good life. I would have to say that our own children have always been more appreciative of what we did for them than I was as a "Boomer" in the 50's and 60's. I have deep regrets about that.

My parents Jack and Hazel (who for reasons unknown to me to this day my brother and I called by their first names) were great parents. Jack was born on July 17, 1919, in Akron, Ohio. He always claimed he was born in Chambersburg, Pennsylvania, where he did indeed grow up, but his birth certificate says, "Born in Akron, Ohio." I'm going with his birth certificate. Hazel was born in Chambersburg, Pennsylvania, on October 2, 1922. I put these birth dates in because throughout my life I never remembered their birthdays.

Jack had begun working on the Western Maryland Railroad after returning from World War II where he served in France. His Army outfit, the 724th Railroad Battalion, Company "C", transported food and supplies to both our soldiers and the allied armies fighting against the German Army. Another regret is never taking the time to ask my father about his experiences during the war. Everyone always said, "Well, it's just something that they did not want to talk about." My suspicion is that many "Boomers" simply took for granted the efforts of their parents during those years. It was something they did but not something of great interest to us. I'm sure there are people of my generation who did take the time to talk with their parents about this period in our history, but for the most part words were not exchanged.

Jack had three brothers: Bob, who like Jack served in the Army, was in WWII the longest and fought at Monte Cassino; and two younger brothers, Pete and Gerald, who both served in the Navy in the Pacific theater. All four brothers saw extensive action in their respective branches of the armed services. They all came home unscathed, which was an amazing accomplishment. The one thing that I recognized and appreciated my entire life is that all the brothers, Jack in particular, looked at their service as something that was required of them. They fought in those wars because it was the right thing to do, and after it was over...it was over. I'm not going to say that they didn't think about it or there weren't emotional scars from what they had been through but they never talked about it and they never expected accolades because they fought in these wars. Their service to our country did not define them. They rarely wore their WWII baseball caps to the grocery store or to public events except if it was a patriotic event that honored those lost in the war. They all went on with their respective lives, had careers that enabled them to take care of their families and raised their kids to be successful, providing opportunities for their children that were never afforded them when they grew up during the Depression. They have made me proud to be an American.

When I went back and reread what I've written here about Jack and his brothers, I realized that I forgot one other family veteran. My Uncle Bob's wife, Ann, my aunt was a Captain in the U.S. Army during World War II. Bob and Ann had two sons, my cousins, Bob and Kip. They too are part of the "Boomer" generation. My cousin Bob who I mentioned earlier in the book, dropped out of college in the late sixties, went to Hawaii and was in the taxi business there and lived in Honolulu for twenty-five years. He came home in the nineties, took care of his ailing father and then in early 2000's went back to Villanova University and not only finished his undergraduate degree in math but then continued and got his Master's degree in math. His brother Kip, joined the United States Marine Corps after college, was a distinguished military lawyer and ultimately retired after thirty years as a Lieutenant Colonel. Their success is directly attributable to their parents wanting them to have a better life than they had had growing up during the Depression.

Getting back to my father Jack, he tried to be the best father that he could to my brother and me. He worked incredibly hard on the Western Maryland Railroad for forty-two years. It was not uncommon for him to get calls at 2:00 am for a job going to Cumberland or Baltimore or some other town or city in the Western Maryland Railroad's region after he had already come home earlier that night at perhaps 8:00 p.m. Jack also had hobbies and skills that he did his best to pass on to me. He learned to cane chairs and refinish furniture. An old high school friend of mine recently sent me a picture on Facebook of a chair that he still has in his home that Jack had refinished and caned for him fifty years ago. Jack gave me every opportunity to engage in his projects and learn his self-taught skills.

I attribute my disinterest in learning these skills for the most part to an undiagnosed attention deficit problem that has haunted me my whole life. I didn't realize that this was an issue until late in my life. Throughout my life I've learned to compensate for the problem, and really, it has all worked out, but nonetheless I wish I would've been able to pay more attention to what Jack was trying to do for me when I was young. I'll have to fall back on the French singer, Edith Piaf's advice: "Non, je ne regrette rien." That is however easier said than done. I wish I had been a bit more attentive in those days. C'est la vie I guess.

I think, though, that the absolute best thing Jack ever did for me was simply being a role model. He was kind, sympathetic and amazingly tolerant of my many indifferences. I never heard him tell a racial joke but he did tell many funny jokes and stories that did not belittle others. He treated others as he would have wanted to be treated. I have always felt honored to be his son.

My mother Hazel was an incredible person as well, and she too allowed me to be myself. She was always looking for something that would engage me when I was a kid. I'd watch some tap-dancing act on "The Ed Sullivan Show" and then try to emulate those dances by tap-dancing down the steps in our house. Hazel mistakenly thought I had potential which sparked the idea of me taking tap-dancing lessons. I remember going to dance class in Williamsport on a Saturday morning and being horrified that I was the only boy in class, as well as suffering my first experience of stage fright. My dancing career came to an abrupt end on that Saturday morning. I think Hazel had our steps carpeted the next week.

I remember having an accordion salesman show up at our house one evening when I was eight or nine to explore my interest in playing the accordion. Looking back, I appreciate Hazel and Jack's efforts on my behalf to help me become a little more culturally enriched, but after one lesson it was pretty clear I wouldn't be dazzling polka fans with a fabulous array of Lederhosen tunes. I've learned recently that my cousin, Bob actually took accordion lessons when he was young and could play this squeeze box of an instrument. Hazel and Jack tried all kinds of things that would open my mind to different experiences and opportunities throughout my growing years, but nothing stuck except maybe basketball, and as much as I grew to love the game, I was never very good at that either, but that became the one thing that provided me with an identity as I moved on in life.

Hazel was very smart. She and Jack got married when she was eighteen. She took care of my brother Skip during the war and held things together on the home front. I have no idea what went through her mind during those times because I never asked, but I know she did what she had to do to maintain the family unit.

She was a housewife for a good part of my early life, maybe up until I was twelve or thirteen. I am smart enough and aware enough as an older person to say that the term "housewife" should never have been trivialized. Housewives were managers, and though they were never compensated for the incredible jobs they did, they were the reason that our families succeeded. That is no small accomplishment.

Hazel was the one with the outgoing sense of humor. She enjoyed jokes. She enjoyed dabbling in funny poems. This is the trait that she passed on me. Like many women of her day, Hazel was not able to go to college. She joined the conventional workforce when I was about twelve or thirteen and worked in the advertising department at *The Herald Mail* Newspaper Company in Hagerstown. Hazel's personality was always a positive infectious motivator for those with whom she worked. Everyone knew Hazel in Hagerstown because of her work at *The Herald Mail*. I have no doubt that she could have climbed corporate ladder had she gotten into the workforce at an earlier age and had a college degree to add to her resumé.

Before entering the professional workforce, Hazel had been a meticulous homemaker. To the best of my very limited research, our house at 38 Roessner Avenue in Halfway, MD, was a "craftsmen" design home. We had four bedrooms and one bathroom on the upper level and a living room, dining room and kitchen on the lower level. I always thought it was pretty nice house, but Hazel made it that way from the furniture that combined new, used and antique décor.

Everything was always neat and blended together flawlessly. Hazel took care of all of this as well as taking care of me, my brother and my father. Hazel was a great cook and always had nutritious, great-tasting meals. She ironed my pants and shirts for school every day. She took care of doctor's appointments, got me well when I was sick, bought me new glasses every time I broke the previous pair or required an upgrade and saw me through all of the emotional highs and lows associated with being an air-headed kid. She was a good caregiver.

Both Jack and Hazel were always supportive of everything I wanted to do, even though I had probably given up on whatever previous thing I wanted to try. Throughout my life they were there for me. Jack died on November 5, 1999, and Hazel passed on February 22, 2007. I think they knew that I appreciated them. I hope they did. I have taken time in my adult life, especially my later adult life, to be there for my wife Cass, my kids Kate, Emma and Michael and my grandchildren Hazel, Mark and Ruth as a way of passing on my parents' unrequited appreciation to my own family.

My brother Skip (Jack Jr.) and I co-existed for a relatively short time. Skip is six years older than me. By the time I was five or six, I had begun to develop my own neighborhood friends, and Skip already had a cohort of friends. Skip was a lot cooler than I was. He had baseball card collections and knew their value. He was mechanically inclined, and prior to being old enough to own and work on cars, he would customize his bikes. I remember that he and one of his friends, Johnny Ott, modified their bikes to include jerry-rigged sets of exhaust pipes. They stuffed them with flammable materials and would ride their bikes with these flames shooting out the back. Hazel thought he and his friends were nuts and she was probably right but I thought the "flame exhaust" was pretty cool. Another modification to bikes to make them sound like they had motors was attaching either balloons or baseball cards with wooden clothes pins in a way that they would cause them to flick against the spokes of the bike and make a motor sound as the bike moved forward. I kind of wonder today if I may have destroyed a lot of valuable baseball cards. Mickey Mantle made a brief rumbling noise and then crumpled into history.

Skip was a much better athlete than me (relatively speaking of course) and I'm sure if he ever reads this he'll agree. He had confidence in his abilities to play sports. I could hold my own in practices or in recreational sports but put a group of spectators in front of me and I was always conscious of making a mistake. At any rate, I recognized our differences. He was an outstanding football and basketball player in high school. I remember seeing clippings of his exploits in the newspaper and envying him.

When I was ten or eleven and Skip was sixteen or seventeen, he began dating and fell in love with a South Hagerstown High School cheerleader named Pam Beranger. Their relationship evolved into a high school marriage. They had three children together and have been married for 63 years as of this writing, so there must have been something there. I'm very proud of Skip and Pam. They have worked so hard for their entire lives, lived in many places and been very successful. They both could have easily gone on to college (Skip, later in life did attend community college), but circumstances didn't allow that; nonetheless, they are models of what families are supposed to be. Skip and I are not exactly close, but we have this unspoken understanding. We enjoy seeing one another on rare occasions and…we're brothers. Neither of us has had to rely on the other over the years for anything, but if something came up that required either of us to help the other, I know we would have.

I thought I'd have completed the family part of this lengthy chapter at this point, but I'm writing this during the Great Pandemic of 2021, so I'll finish up with a bit of humor. Humor most certainly played an important part in the life of our family. If we were sitting around watching a comedian on television, maybe on "The Ed Sullivan Show," there would always be some comic who told a story that would make us laugh so hard we'd cry. I especially loved seeing Hazel and Jack succumb to hysterical laughter.

Jack was a fan of Crazy Guggenheim, played by comedian Frank Fontaine, and he really liked the Jewish comedian Myron Cohen, who would come up with these dry-witted stories that made Jack laugh out loud. Hazel was more of a Jack Benny and Rochester (played by Eddie Anderson) enthusiast. When Jack and Hazel laughed to where they had tears in their eyes, it would make me laugh just as hard.

There are also a couple of family stories that have been repeated many times over throughout my life but none-the-less cause family members to emit a chuckle or two. Here are two that give some insight into my generational humor.

My father Jack told the following story, and he too would laugh every single time he told it. Now, before I commence, allow me to warn you. If you're a pet lover this story may be upsetting. My grandmother's sister, my great-aunt May, ran a boarding house across the street from the Western Maryland Railroad in the west end of Hagerstown. I assume that single male railroaders would stay there for periods of time awaiting work orders for jobs on the freight trains that provided a lot of employment for Hagerstown residents, including my father and two of his four brothers. May had a boarder by the name of John Rogers, who I think doubled as May's husband. I have a gold watch that belonged to John that he had given to my father, and when Jack died, he willed it to me, so I guess there was a family connection. John lived in the boarding house, and he too worked on the Western Maryland Railroad.

The year of the incident that I'm about to relate is unknown, but I guess it occurred in the late 40's or early 50's. John was apparently a grizzly old soul, and like many of his generation he had grown up during the Great Depression. Food was a precious commodity during the Depression years. As the story goes, one morning John came down for breakfast before going to work. He poured himself some corn flakes into a bowl and then went to the refrigerator to search for some milk. There was a bottle of milk in the fridge with just enough milk for his cereal. He came back, sat down and poured the milk into the cereal bowl before realizing that nature was calling, so he went to the bathroom. When he came back to his breakfast, he immediately noticed that there was no longer any milk in his bowl. Glancing to the other end of the table, he saw the house cat sitting there licking his paws, having just finished the milk in John's bowl. Without hesitation John got up from the table, went to a bureau drawer in the room next to the kitchen, found his gun, came back out and shot the cat. My apologies to cat-lovers. Times were a bit different in those days.

Before I get started on the next story, my brother Skip will be thinking, "My God, he's told me this story a thousand times," and while that may indeed be true, you haven't heard it. When Hazel would tell this story it always brought tears to her eyes, which made the story worth hearing over and over again. My grandmother Mick (Jack's mother) had three sisters, May, Dos and Sis, and at least one brother. All four of the sisters were pushing 6' tall, and all of their husbands were about 5'6". Their size has nothing to do with the story, but I find this to be an interesting fact. The story is about Sis, with a minor acting role from my grandmother Mick, who played an important part because she was the person who recounted this charade.

Sis's brother was a little older and apparently picked on his younger sister a lot, probably in a mischievous way rather than a mean way. On the day that this incident took place, Sis and Mick (young girls then) were playing on the second floor of their house. Sis happened to look out the window and saw her brother down below playing in the grass. What sparked Sis to think of this remains a mystery, but she had a handkerchief with her, and for whatever reason she squatted and pooped in the handkerchief and said to her astonished sister, "Watch this." Sis stuck her head back out of the window and called to her brother, "Hey, I bet you can't catch this!" and she held this neatly folded "aromatic" pouch out the window to show him. "Whatever that is, I can catch it." "No, you can't," she said. "Throw it down!" She did and he caught it! What ensued after that can only be left to your imagination, but be assured that a lot of yelling and chasing was involved.

## Junior High School

The foundation of my formal education most certainly occurred in elementary school. I don't recall having a particular difficulty with any subject. My attention deficit issues were not apparent to me then, nor were they until I was in my 60's, but looking back, junior high school is where my inability to focus hit me like a brick.

I went to South Potomac Junior High School from 1959 to 1961. In seventh grade it became apparent to me that I had some challenges ahead of me. Math and science require having to equate symbols with numbers. There was no way I could do that on my own, and the teachers that I had, although they may have been good for students who had the ability to focus, were not aware or prepared to handle my deficiencies. There were no teachers' assistants or opportunities during or after class to reinforce the subjects in a way that I could understand what was being taught. I went through the motions and did what I had to do to pass a course. Passing a test "may" have involved a bit of cheating. This, was simply a survival technique that I had to incorporate into my daily classes in order to pass and move on to the next year. I wasn't insightful enough at that time to realize any of this. I was twelve or thirteen years old, and that was how I had to approach my education during those years.

The seventh grade was the first year I took the bus to school. When I got off the bus on many mornings, I would run out of the parking lot to the intersection of South Potomac Street and Marsh Run, cross the street and run down to Hartle's Deli on South Potomac Street to purchase a Hartle's Original Cold-Cut Hot Sub. The Original was an

Italian submarine sandwich (never to be confused with a "Hoagie"). This is still (arguably) the best Italian cold-cut sub in the world. Why it is, remains a mystery to me. The ingredients are Bologna, white American cheese, tomatoes, and a mountain of sliced white onions, all doused with a hot red pepper sauce on a soft, white submarine roll. I mean, that's it, but no one in Hagerstown history has ever been able to replicate this sandwich in another deli or in their home. There's no explanation for it, but it is just the best submarine sandwich. You could buy a whole Original for $ 0.60 or a half for $ 0.35. I only had enough for half, and that was only on certain days when I had saved my milk money from previous on-site school lunches. When you got one of these sandwiches back to school, you'd put it in your locker, and all you could think about was lunchtime when you could open your locker and be knocked over by this hot, spicy smell that ramped up your taste buds to unprecedented levels. I would like to note here that recently, in 2021, I took a nostalgic trip to Hagerstown and I stopped at Hartle's Sub Shop for an original Hartle's Italian sub and bill for the sub and a Pepsi was $11.35. I'm generally not one that longs for the good old days but this may have been one of those days when inflation caused me to look back with nostalgia.

One thing that gave me a little semblance of normalcy and acceptance was playing in the South Potomac Junior High School "Bulldog" marching band. In elementary school everyone was encouraged to play an instrument. I couldn't read or learn (at least I thought I couldn't) to read music, so my instrument of choice was the drums. My brother played drums, so that was another consideration for signing on to the percussion section. When I got to junior high school, I joined the band.

Playing snare drums required a bit more than muscle memory and an intuitive natural rhythm. You had to read music. Fortunately, the music director was not as concerned about the percussion section as he was with the brass and woodwinds. In class I would just sort of wing it to the best of my ability. The marching band had room for only so many snare drummers and I was not one of them. I chose the bass drum mainly because none of the rest of the drummers had a particular interest in playing it. I excelled as a bass drummer, and honestly it was easier to carry than having those snare drums bounce against your leg causing pain and bruising throughout the marching band season, which started in September and ended by marching in the "marginally-famous" Alsatia Mummer's Parade on Halloween in Hagerstown. This is the biggest annual event in Hagerstown. 2021 will mark the 100th anniversary of the parade. When it gets right down to it, in the marching band I couldn't really screw up too badly playing the bass drum. I'm relatively sure that if there was a "Hall-of-Fame" for junior high school bass drum players, there's a chance I would be in it or least on the honorable-mention list.

I also played in the "B" symphony band. Imagine—there were that many not-so-good student musicians that a "B" band symphony could be formed. I guess that most of these B band musicians could read music but either couldn't play their respective instrument particularly well, or else reading and responding to what they read was somewhat difficult and always left them a half-note behind. I, on the other hand, did not concern myself with interpreting sheets of music. I was a "B" band percussionist after all. Intuitively, I could bang the drum with the best of them. The highlight of my much-too-short bass drum career was having a key part in George Gershwin's "Summertime." As you musicologists may remember, there are several times during the piece that call for crashing thunder from the bass drum and cymbals, which I flawlessly incorporated into my thundering on my bass drum as directed by the orchestra leader. My thunderous booms and crashing cymbal sounds brought the house down, so much so that I saw audience members leaving to seek shelter or maybe a smoke break.

There is not much else to reflect on during these torturous two years in my life, but there was one more thing. I consider myself to be relatively smart (despite my inability to cope with math and science).

Other than my brief encounter with the Black kid at the Y.M.C.A. when I was younger, South Potomac Junior High School was my first exposure to African-American students. I never had any problems with Black kids, and that was in part because I never really knew any before junior high school and because my parents never made differences an issue. I don't want to say that these students were a curiosity to me, but it wasn't until later in life that I wondered what must have been going through their minds in those times. How did they cope with being viewed as different? They had no choice but to be there and make the best of their situation, which meant always being noticed but never really being a part of things. I wonder what teachers thought of having Black students in their class. This was 1960. Public schools throughout the country were still struggling with integration. I don't recall teachers being biased against Black students and I hope they weren't.

There was one daily occurrence that has stuck in my mind to this day. Arthur Gaines, who I later played basketball with at South Hagerstown High School, worked in the school cafeteria lunchroom every day while he was a student at the school. I can only guess he did that as an accommodation by school officials to provide him with a lunch every day which was a quarter for lunch and a nickel for milk. That was $.30 his parents simply may have not had. Even then I kind of felt for him, but it was beyond my attention-deficit mind to ask why.

When I moved on to high school, Arthur was a team-mate and much better basketball player than me. I never took the time to befriend Arthur, even though he was a teammate.

I remember seeing that Art died a few years ago. I looked up his obituary in Hagerstown. He died in 2016. He was a Vietnam Veteran. He had a family who loved him. He appears to have had a good life. I sincerely hope that was the case. I greatly regret never having the insight or willingness to know him as a friend. I would have liked to ask him all of these questions about what it was like to be Black in Hagerstown.

That was the gist of my two-year stint at South Potomac Junior High School. Go Bulldogs! Before moving on to high school I think a brief history of Hagerstown is needed to provide the viewers with a sense of the kind of place it was.

## Hagerstown

Hagerstown, known as the "Home of the Flying Boxcar," was a great little city in which to grow up. In my youth in the 50's and 60's, Hagerstown was the second- largest city in Maryland. It looked like a city. Old photos of downtown Hagerstown depict heavy traffic composed of cars and buses, sidewalks full of people, men in suits and ties wearing fedoras, fashion-conscious women wearing fancy hats and carrying pocketbooks, trolley cars and large buildings and department stores. You could take a passenger train from Hagerstown and go to Chicago or New York. If you would show a photo of Hagerstown in its heyday to someone unfamiliar with the town, they would assume they were seeing pictures of Baltimore, New York or Chicago.

Incidentally, the "Flying Box Car" was an incredibly serviceable supply transport plane. I remember these planes very well in the 50's. They would fly over our backyard at least a couple of times a day at a height that I guess was no more than 1,000 feet. It was as advertised, this giant box-like aircraft that was 84 feet from front to back with a wing-span of 108 feet and a bubble-like body that had two tail wings. It could carry about 35,000 lbs. and could ascend to a height of 24,000 feet.

Besides being known as "Home of the Flying Boxcar," Hagerstown also attained an infamous reputation as "Little Chicago." It was a bustling little city, and with 10,000 Fairchild workers who all had a lot of money to spend, there were stories that at least some of this discretionary income was spent in nefarious ways, which may have included gambling, prostitution and related boosts to the city's economy. I'm just speculating here based on stories that I heard growing up in Hagerstown, mind you, but when you see photos and footage of this era, it's not hard to imagine that Hagerstown could've indeed have been "Chi Town" in miniature.

Eyerly's Department Store on Washington Street was comparable to any big city department store of that era and it was the high-end store of all the other stores. It had elevators. It had those old vacuum-type tubes in the ceiling that were used to suck messages, money, bills, whatever through them, and they'd end up in some office, their destination known only to the staff who collected the contents of the tubes at the end of each journey.

The elevator in those days was operated by African-Americans. As a kid I remember going into Eyerly's Department Store with Hazel, and the Black woman who operated the elevator knew my mother's name. Honestly, it seemed to me that she knew everyone's name who ascended to the different levels of the building, and they in turn knew her name. It always seemed to me that my mother was very respectful of this lady and vice-versa. Those kinds of interactions emanating from your parents stick in your memory. You learned that respecting others regardless of your differences was important. That was my experience, but that may have not been the case for other customers.

Hagerstown had three movie theaters on the same block of South Potomac Street, the street up from the "Square." The Square was the main intersection of Washington Street (Route 11) and North and South Potomac Streets (Route 40). All of the heavy traffic downtown intersected at the Square. It was a busy hub. Besides the previously mentioned Eyerly's, there were Leiter's Department Store, F.W. Woolworth's, J.J. Newberry's, McCrory's, Rosen's (which sold Jack

Purcell sneakers or "fish heads" but not Converse All-Stars), Glick Shoes, Thom McCann Shoes and Ingram's Men's Store.

There was kind of a hierarchy of stores and depending on how much money you had to spend or particular need. On the Square or near were restaurants, Hewitt's Bakery and People's Drug Store. The "Square" was the center piece of the town. From the time I was eleven or twelve years old, I would go to the Y.M.C.A. in Hagerstown one night a week and on Saturday mornings. People's Drug Store was my destination bus stop after taking either the Halfway Bus or Williamsport bus on Virginia Avenue into town. There were also these "fly-by-night" novelty stores, like Hill's Novelty Store that was next to Henry's Theater. Cromer's was another such store on East Franklin Street but Hill's was special. Hill's Store was the mecca of toys that kids really liked but as time went on disappeared from the shelves for fear of bodily injury. Hill's had sling shots, BB guns, bows and arrows, pea shooters, cap guns along with an incredible assortment of puzzles, magic tricks and games. They sold live dyed-purple, orange and green baby chicks at Easter; all things that would spark the imagination of any kid were available in this magical emporium.

The theaters were special. As mentioned, there were three, The Colonial, Henry's and the Maryland Theater. These were not theaters that were created from reconfigured large row houses, as was the case in smaller towns. These were real luxurious theaters with balconies, plush seats and large screens. You could have physically moved the Maryland and Colonial Theaters to a big city, and they would fit right in. On Friday and Saturday nights there would be lines of people around the block hoping to get tickets. If you were towards the end of the line for the Maryland or the Colonial and no more tickets were available, you'd settle for Henry's Theatre that was smaller but still had the amenities of the other movie houses. I think that right after the war, things were just like…in the movies. Life had new meaning and the prospect for a better future was within reach.

Hagerstown had three downtown hotels in its heyday, The Hamilton, the Alexander Hotel which was the grandest of the three and the Dagmar. The Alexander is a ten-story hotel that could rival any hotel in a city like Baltimore. It is still the tallest building in Hagerstown. With the demise of downtown as suburbia took hold, the Alexander became a "dinosaur." Tourism ceased to exist. Somewhere along the line the hotel was turned over to Social Services and became an affordable housing complex for older people and people with disabilities. This is certainly a good use for the building, but it always fascinates me in 2021 when I make a rare visit to Hagerstown that the main Square on which the Alexander sits is now inhabited by an army of people in wheelchairs and on walkers.

The Dagmar Hotel was unique in my time for two reasons: Danny Litton, a classmate of mine in junior high school and I used to play basketball on the sixth floor of the hotel. His father owned the hotel as I recall and there was a large ballroom on the sixth floor with exposed ceiling beams and we'd shoot hoops at one spot on a particular beam to score points. We would drive what few tenants the hotel had, nuts. The other distinguishing feature of the Dagmar was that during my high school years and slightly beyond, they turned the Dagmar into a residence for medical secretarial students, all of whom were young women just out of high school. The Dagmar was a focal point for many a young man in and around Hagerstown during the mid-sixties and early seventies. Their interests of course were medicinal.

Fairchild Industries, an American aircraft and aerospace manufacturing company, employed 10,000 people at the height of its production heyday, a third of Hagerstown's population at that time. My mother told me this story about my Uncle Bob. He had returned to Hagerstown after serving two-and-a-half years in Italy in WWII. When he returned, he began working again at the Western Maryland Railroad, which had been required by law to hold the jobs of Uncle Bob as well as my father until they returned from the war. At that time the Nicodemus

Bank in Hagerstown was the largest bank in the city. Their primary customers were employees from Fairchild Aircraft. On Friday nights these employees (I'm assuming though not all 10,000 of them) would go to the Nicodemus Bank to cash their checks and for their other personal transactions.

Uncle Bob also was a Nicodemus Bank customer. He too decided to go to the bank on Friday. When he got to the teller, the teller said to him, "I'm sorry, Mr. Naugle, but we only serve Fairchild employees on Friday night." Now, this is a man who was known to have a bit of a short temper to begin with, and also, he had risked his life every single day for the previous two and a half years fighting against German soldiers while the Fairchild employees, who most certainly contributed to the war effort by helping to build fighter planes, risked nothing, made very good money and were privileged enough to be able to go home at night to their families. As the story goes. Bob exploded! It was one of those "you could hear a pin drop" moments when he said, and I can only paraphrase, "I just spent three years in North Africa and Italy fighting the worst sons of bitches on the face of the earth. You will cash my check right now!" They cashed his check.

There are so many memorable stories about Hagerstown that I could share, but if you want to know more, you have to read the book. (Do you remember that "cop out" when you were in grade school?) My classmates and I were required to read a book, and then at some point during the week you were required to stand up in front of your classmates and give a report on the book that you had read that week. I wasn't alone in hardly ever reading the book, but you'd capture enough about the book's contents and you'd provide some general, random comment, make that comment last as long as possible and then unabashedly say, "And if you want to know more, you have to read the book." Obviously, the teacher would roll her eyes and imply, "Next time, please read the book." I believe I may have gone off topic here. Back to Hagerstown.

In 1974 the Valley Mall opened in Hagerstown. I had not lived in Hagerstown for about seven years at that time. The opening of this mall was the demise of downtown Hagerstown as I had remembered it from my youth. There was no more foot traffic. Parking had always been an issue but now you could find a parking spot in front of what had been your favorite store, but the store was no longer there. Movie theaters soon closed. You could go to the mall, find an easy parking space, go into the mall and be protected from inclement weather, shop if you wanted to before going to see one of a number of movies available to you, all in one building.

Fast-forward fifty years and downtown Hagerstown is still a shell of itself. If you drive up North Prospect Street towards City Park, stop your car and look out over the town, it still looks like a real city. It's very picturesque but there's not much there. It will take great vision and major investment to turn Hagerstown around. "Gentrification" may be the only way to revitalize downtown Hagerstown. In 2021 affordable housing is a major issue throughout our country. Rehabbing the many beautiful old buildings in the city of Hagerstown and turning them into "truly" affordable apartments and condominiums may be the only solution to revive a once thriving city.

## Begin the Beguine

South Hagerstown High School was a six-year-old very contemporary place of higher learning when I began my freshman year there in 1961. High school is something that most of us look forward to, but for many different reasons. I'm not sure how I felt about it. First of all, you had to decide what course you wanted to take. I don't have a clue as to what records or recommendations are made on your behalf by the previous school you attended, which in my case was South Potomac Junior High School. I can't think of anything I did well academically during those two years, so my suspicion is that my recommendation said, "Michael should be in the General course. He seems a bit slow." Right from the "get go" there's this peer pressure to want to be in the Academic curriculum. In my case, I really didn't have that option and I would've in all likelihood flunked out of high school in my freshman year. I certainly didn't want to be in the shop courses. I mean, girls would probably think I was stupid. (They wouldn't have been too far off.)

Much, much later in life I realized how valuable those shop courses were, probably more so than the academic courses. When my car needs repairs or if my plumbing or electricity is messed up, my fellow students who were in those courses are the ones who come to my house, charge me $65.00 when they walk in the door, fix my leaky faucet, give me a bill for $300.00 and I'm happy to pay it. One of my childhood friends in Hagerstown took Body Shop at South High. Rumor has it that he's now a millionaire in Hagerstown and has one of the best-known car repair businesses in the Hagerstown region.

I thought it would sound cool for me to take the Commercial course. I associated that with business and figured that would be an admirable path to a great future, and it was something I could defend if my course of action was criticized by my academic friends. I took courses like bookkeeping, business math (no equations necessary), business law and typing. From an academic standpoint (well, I guess a commercial standpoint technically), typing was undoubtedly the most useful course that I took in high school. Typing really is responsible for my creative writing (and to some the word "creative" is a relative term), but I could never have written school papers, letters, dumb poetry, any of that if I had not been introduced to typing. It's one of those lifetime skills. I can't help but think that some of you who are suffering to stay with this autobiography are saying to yourself, "I wish he would've taken shop."

My freshman year at South High was uneventful. I think everyone just tries to find their place or identity. Sports were my only option, and I wasn't a stellar athlete. I think in my freshman year I was 6'1" tall and I weighed about 135 lbs. I was not interested in football, not because of my skeletal frame, but because there was no way I was going to give up the latter part of my summer vacation to start football practice, where you're expected to show up in the mornings and afternoons in 90-degree temperatures and be subjected to deranged coaches screaming at you while suffering through difficult and degrading exercises and their incessant verbal humiliation. Playing football in somebody's backyard in the fall months was a blast, but putting yourself through this August torture, knowing that you might not even play in the game—no. I was skinny and somewhat of a wuss, but I wasn't stupid.

I knew basketball was the only thing that would give me some kind of an identity in this world of upperclassmen who lorded it over you for being a dumb freshman, or at least that's what I thought. I went out for the junior varsity team and was cut on the first day. I was devastated but at the same time somewhat relieved because the junior varsity coach in my mind was an over-the-top task-master. He had a reputation of being really hard on his players so that they could be prepared to take future abuse from Nick Scallion, the varsity coach. Some kids are able to cope with abuse in a way that doesn't damage them psychologically. Others, like me specifically, did not respond well to these boot-camp instructional tactics. I spent that fall and winter playing basketball at the YMCA having fun and not being ridiculed.

## White Men Can Jump (Who Da Thunk?)

My sophomore year went a little better, as I hoped it would. At the very least, I had passed my freshman year. My YMCA basketball nights had provided me with an unusual and unexpected ability. I could jump. I had grown a bit and my weight had ballooned up to about 140 lbs. When you're in a gym like the Y, you're always messing around and trying new things. I remember jumping up to see if I could touch the rim of the basket. Each attempt got me a little closer. It became a repetitive activity until one night I was able to jump and hang on to the rim. I think I spent the rest of that night just running, jumping and hanging on the rim. It was an epiphany of sorts. In those days dunking was somewhat of an anomaly.

There are several things of interest that happened, most of which are sports-related, but there was one surreal occurrence during my sophomore year that altered my obliviousness to national or world events. I was sitting in Mr. Eyler's Civics class, eyes half-glazed over as usual, and this startling announcement came over the intercom. I believe it was Mr. Richard Whisner, Principal of the school, who prepared us for this. "Ladies and gentlemen, I am so sorry to inform you that our President, John F. Kennedy has been assassinated." It was an announcement that left me and my fellow students in a state of shock. As sons and daughters of the "Greatest Generation" I think we were insulated from the harsh realities of the world. The possibility of something like this happening in our lifetime was unimaginable. We just sat there speechless, not knowing what to say. I seem to remember that we were released from school early on that day. I think Kennedy's death in a convoluted sort of way made me aware of impending adulthood. Every time I see historical footage of that day, I am reminded of where I was on that day almost sixty-years ago when I heard this terrible news.

On the sports front, my jumping ability along with my height gave me enough credence with Joe Robeson, the new junior varsity basketball coach, that I made the team. That was a big deal for me. Robeson had taken over the junior varsity coaching job from the authoritarian Mr. Hicks, who knowingly or unknowingly effected the psyche of many aspiring young players. Robeson had a normal demeanor. He understood that different players respond to criticism in different ways, and he adjusted his coaching skills, strategies and practices to the abilities of his players. As a result, this was a fun year for me. I was not a starter, but I played and felt as if I made a contribution to the team. Robeson referred to me as "George Mikan." Mikan was one of the first skilled big men in the NBA. He played in the 50's for the Minneapolis Lakers (who later moved to Los Angeles). He was 6'10" tall, and looking at old photographs of him I can see the resemblance. He was certainly much taller than me but was gangly, had short hair and wore glasses, which I did in my sophomore year. He made a whole lot more money than me.

South High played in the Tri-State League, which included teams from Maryland, Pennsylvania and West Virginia, all of which were close to Hagerstown. On that level we had a pretty good team and found ourselves playing against the Martinsburg Bulldog junior varsity team for the league championship that year, which I think was in 1963. The game was in Martinsburg and preceded the varsity game. We were pretty evenly matched, so much so that the game ended in a tie in regulation time, which was also the outcome at the end of the first overtime and the second overtime; however, the third overtime was the charm. We were tied in the closing seconds and for some inexplicable reason, I was in the game. As the clocked ticked down to the last three seconds of the three-minute overtime period, an errant rebound came my way on the offensive end. My intention was to grab the rebound, but reaching out with my left hand I inadvertently slapped at the ball and it went up towards the hoop and banked in for the winning basket. Tri-state Champions—albeit junior varsity. My name of course appeared in an article in the Hagerstown *Morning Herald* the next day, which described how deftly I had put the winning shot in with my left hand. (Again, I'm paraphrasing here a bit.)

After the basketball season was over and bolstered by my newly-acclaimed athleticism, I went out for track and field. My friend Dave Zook and I tried everything but settled on the high hurdles for God knows what reason. High hurdles are a skilled discipline. They require speed and the ability not only to get over each hurdle without hitting it with your foot, falling and almost killing yourself but also to take three giant steps in between hurdles that are spaced about 28 feet apart. Neither Zook nor I had speed, and our hurdling ability was suspect. We thought we had pretty good form, but as hard as we tried, we always took five steps between hurdles. A good time for the 100-yard-high hurdles when we were in high school was between 14 and 15 seconds. Our best times were between 19 and 20 seconds with a strong tail-wind. Zook and I were very competitive, but only against one another.

We went to a meet at the Mercersburg Academy in Mercersburg, Pennsylvania, in the spring of 1963. It was an historical event in our eyes—not to anyone else. For whatever reason, conditions were perfect. The track was solidly packed, unlike the cinder-ridden track at South Hagerstown. It was a lovely sun-filled afternoon, and we were ready to showcase our skills to the track world. The race started and we were off. The hurdling gods were on our side that day. We took three steps between every single hurdle. I was winning, although to this day Zook insists that he won, but at the next-to-last hurdle Zook hit the hurdle and tumbled to the ground. On the other hand, I raced like the wind and won the race with a time of 17.6 seconds, easily the best time of my brief but storied hurdling career. My name was in *The Morning Herald* the next day as finishing first at the Mercersburg Invitational. My name was even mentioned at morning announcements the next day. I retired from hurdling after that race knowing that I crushed Zook in our first and final showdown. I could mention this to Zook today and he would still claim that he won, even though he fell over the hurdle.

During that spring track and field season I did accidentally find an event where I could excel. My newly discovered jumping ability allowed me to succeed at the high jump. I had no technique other than the scissor jump. The scissor jump is simply jumping off your strong foot and leg, kicking the opposite leg up in the air followed by the foot and leg you jumped off, bending your back, raising your butt and clearing the bar, assuming you're successful. I started jumping in junior varsity meets and always finished 1st, 2nd, or 3rd and reached decent heights of 5'6" to 5'8".

At the end of my junior year of basketball, I was exhausted and decided not to go out for track. I just thought it would be nice to go home from school every day at the normal time. I started messing around again with the high jump in gym class, and the football and track coach said I could come out again for the team, but I'd have to start at a junior varsity meet. I went to Boonsboro for a junior varsity meet and jumped 5'11." That was a decent jump at that time for a varsity meet but unheard of for a junior varsity meet. That was a record that stood for twenty-five years, and when it was broken my mother said she saw in *The Morning Herald* that my record had been broken. Surely, it must've been a misprint.

I did jump 6' in both my junior and senior years. In my senior year I finished 6th in the state, which I guess was some kind of accomplishment. The guy who won that year jumped 6'3" and he scissored. I've never seen anyone else jump that high with that technique. He was also white, which again proves that white men can jump—as long as they scissor jump.

## An Ounce of Prevention Is Worth a Pound of Flesh

As mentioned, I made the varsity basketball team in my junior year. Being on the basketball team established an identity for me. Making a high school basketball team even then was not easy. A varsity team was usually composed of twelve players, and to get through try-outs and be picked for the squad was no small accomplishment. By my junior year I had jettisoned up to 6'3," and my weight increased to about 150 lbs. I was a specimen to be sure (in more ways than one). My deft left-handed game winner in the Tri-State championship of the previous season was not what swayed coach Nick Scallion's interest in me. It was my ability to dunk a basketball with relative ease that attracted his attention. I also had an innate ability to block shots (imagine being born with such a skill). In addition to my gazelle-like leaping abilities, I had long arms which added to my defensive prowess.

I played sporadically but did make some contributions to the team here and there. My biggest success was always before the start of each game when I would relentlessly dunk balls in pre-game lay-ups. The crowd went wild! As for the games, I averaged 4 points a game throughout my junior and senior years, which didn't attract the attention of college basketball scouts. In addition to having the distinction of dunking basketballs during the pre-game warm-ups, I should note that I had one other dubious achievement at the end of my senior year. I was chosen as an Honorable Mention All-City basketball team member in *The Herald Mail* newspapers. Butch Plank from St. Maria Goretti also received this "honor." In a city like Baltimore with a lot of high schools this would be somewhat of an honor, but since there were only three high schools in the city, that means that a first, second and third team were selected before the honorable mention designation. Fifteen players from three different teams were chosen before Butch and me. I don't know how Butch felt but I felt a little embarrassed.

Being in the Commercial course did not dismiss me from taking the general academic courses that were required of everyone, regardless of their interests. I had some form of English in all four years of high school. My junior year English class was made more challenging because I was assigned to Madeline Noll's English literature class. She had a "rep" that all South High students knew well. She suffered no fools (which I was until then). She was an excellent teacher and was passionate about the subject that she taught. She also wanted her students to share her passion, and if humiliating you in a way that would make you seem like an absolute moron in front of your classmates… well, she had her ways, and I quickly learned that it was in my best interests to respect this lady. The first half of the school year was devoted to Shakespeare and more specifically to "The Merchant of Venice." She had us listen to vinyl recordings of the exploits of Portia, Shylock and Bassanio, and then she'd quiz us to see if we were listening and comprehending (something with which I had great difficulty). For the first time in my academic career, I was actually engaged in this Shakespearean drama, of all things. A light bulb went off when I understood the "pound of flesh" decision. I was thinking, "Damn, Shakespeare's a pretty clever writer." I remember Miss Noll giving students an option of doing a report on "The Merchant of Venice" or doing a poster; one that could be used in Shakespeare's time to advertise his play. Knowing that writing a report that might require research, I chose the latter. As I remember, I thought my poster was pretty good. Miss Noll gave me a B- and while I may have received higher grades in art or physical education, I was more-proud of that grade than any grade I received in high school. I felt a sense of academic achievement the end of my junior year; the first in many a moon.

## Good Fences Make Good Neighbors

In the summer between my junior year and senior year, I got a job with a company called Regal Fence. Now let me say right up front that the Regal Fence Company, as far as I know, is a very reputable company that I'm sure does excellent fencing jobs throughout the tri-state area of Maryland, Pennsylvania and West Virginia. The following story happened over fifty-five years ago.

The company had a contract with the federal government to put up protective fencing on a five-mile stretch on both sides of I-81 between Williamsport, Maryland, and the Potomac River Bridge that separates Maryland from West Virginia. The purpose of the fencing was to keep animals, in particular deer, from running out in front of cars and trucks and becoming road kill, not to mention people being killed if the deer flew through a windshield upon impact. Unbeknownst to those who were hired to dig holes for fence posts was that the managers of the Regal Fence job were fundamentalist Christians. Now, I'm not one to question one's religious beliefs, but the owners Marvin and Charles were a bit on the fervent side, and their fervency sometimes carried over into the workplace. To their credit they hired a boatload of local teenage students from area high schools (including me) to dig holes for $1.45 an hour during the summer of 1964. Coincidentally I had dug holes the previous summer beside I-81 for a tree company from Norristown, Pennsylvania. I was an experienced hole digger. I could wield a digging iron with the best of them. Among those who were a part of the work force that summer besides me were Tom Stough, Chip Dorsey, Pokey Gilbert, Jerry O'Neil, my cousin Bob and another of his old Hamilton Park acquaintances, Frank Connelly. There were many others whose names I have forgotten, so I'll concentrate my stories on some of the aforementioned employees.

Marvin and Charles worked us like a prison road gang; at least that's how we interpreted our experience as sixteen- and seventeen-year-olds. Our jobs were primarily to dig holes in areas that machines could not access. After the fence posts were set in the holes and filled with concrete, we'd unroll bales of fence and secure the fence to the poles. These bales of fence stretched to about twenty yards (I think), and when we workers set the fence up against the poles, there had to be some teamwork to ensure that the fence didn't collapse and roll down the line where your colleagues were cautiously holding up their section of fence or goofing off and cracking jokes. If you weren't paying attention when others weren't holding up their end of the deal, the fence could roll and wave down the line and slam you into the ground. Fortunately, this did not happen often, but when it did it was a source of amusement for all in attendance except for Marvin and Charles.

Marvin, who was kind of a "good 'old boy,'," as I recall had one of those floating eyes, the kind where you weren't quite sure if he was looking at you or looking at something else. He in particular was always looming around, anticipating that some of us were not pulling our weight, and he certainly had cause. If he wasn't around, nothing got done; but we were very ingenious in how we spent those rare moments free of Marvin's oversight.

Frank Connelly was a skinny little guy who went to St. Maria Goretti High School in Hagerstown. I didn't know Frank until we bonded as prison gang workers on the Regal job. One afternoon Tom Stough and I were standing around, keeping an eye out for Marvin, and someone threw a clump of clay dirt that landed precariously close to Tom. Without flinching Tom picked up a large piece of dirt and threw it at someone who he suspected had thrown dirt at him. Now, Frank was about fifty yards away from us and started getting in on the action, lobbing a clump of dirt back in our direction which hit me in the leg. The dirt war was on, and everyone began hurling lumps of dirt at one another. Tom and I could escape being hit by others except for Frank. Frank could throw a piece of dirt from forty or fifty yards away, and you could see this missile coming at you, and you should've been able to avoid being hit—but no matter how much you dodged Frank's tosses, he hit you in the back. We finally had to enforce a truce for fear of permanent bodily damage. I don't know if Frank played baseball at Goretti. If not, he wasted an opportunity for greatness. If he could pitch a baseball the way he threw clay dirt clumps, he most assuredly would've been in the Catholic League Hall of Fame.

If there was ever a Regal Fence Hall of Fame, one of my work colleagues, Pokey would most assuredly been in it. Pokey grew up in Halfway. He was a smarmy kind of guy. He had thick black hair, and he appeared to have had a beard from the time he was twelve years old. I'm relatively sure that If Pokey shaved in the morning, his 5 o'clock shadow would be in full beard regalia by 9:00 p.m. that night. I have to admit, as a kid I kept my distance from Pokey. He always appeared to me to be a very self-confident person. His reputation was that you did not want to provoke him; you just wanted to co-exist with him; but he also had some redeeming qualities.

Connie White was a schoolmate of mine whose family lived in the neighborhood. Connie had a brother, Warney who was developmentally disabled and may have been on the autism spectrum. Warney's parents were great. They allowed him to roam the neighborhood as he was growing up, and everyone knew Warney. His special autistic ability was remembering your birthday. Once he asked you when you were born, he would never forget it. Years would go by and you'd spot Warney one day in the neighborhood and you'd ask him, "Warney, do you still remember my birthday?" Without hesitating he'd tell you. Warney frequented the Southside Bowling Alley quite often in his youth. His family actually lived right behind the bowling alley. Pokey knew Warney, and he always looked out for him. If someone came into the bowling alley and made fun of Warney, it was the last time they did so, and probably the last time they came into the bowling alley.

Tom Stough relayed a story me that I either forgot or wasn't a part of at the time. Pokey cut his finger on a piece of wire fencing and yelled, "Jesus f_ _king Christ!" Marvin came over to counsel him and suggested that he not use blasphemy, but instead say "Praise the Lord" if he incurred another painful accident. Several minutes later Pokey again cut his finger and shouted, "Praise the f_ _king Lord!" Marvin shook his head and slowly walked away, no doubt feeling sorry that Pokey would surely go to Hell.

Chip (No last names here) is the other Regal Hall-of-Famer of note. I had known Chip since grade school. I remember that when he was in the fourth grade and I was in the third, he bullied me day after day until one day he came up to me, and with all of my might I punched him in the stomach so hard that he doubled over. He never bothered me after that, and even though he was always a pain, but we got along.

He was also a really good baseball player. I threw that in to say something nice about him, but he was a good player and he would tell you as much. He also had this dry sadistic sense of humor that would piss you off sometimes but at other times you'd laugh at some comment he made. Back to the Regal Fence story. Chip was easily the laziest worker among us and the most sadistically funny. He didn't even act like he was working. Why he wasn't fired remains a mystery, but he remained among us for I guess the entire summer.

If we were working on the south side of I-81, in order to get back over to the other side, we had to ride in the back of a pick-up truck over the Potomac River Bridge that separates Maryland from West Virginia. Our tools were also loaded into the back of the truck. If the "Chipper" was riding with us, every time we made the U-turn in West Virginia to come back over the bridge, he would toss some tools over the bridge into the river. If any of those tools had hit a fisherman below, I probably wouldn't be writing this account of that time and place. Chip also coined the Regal Cheer. It would be a calm, hot and damp morning, and everyone was dreading the day ahead, and he would give his Regal Cheer. It was like an intense pig squeal. He would stand there and go ReeeeEEEEEGAL! And we would all stand there and laugh our asses off every time he did it. I know it sounds stupid, and it was, but you just had to be there to gain the full appreciation. Years and years later, those among us who remember working that summer will emit the Regal cheer and we'll all bust out laughing.

This was the summer of our introduction into the working world. I don't know how much insight we gained, but it was a memorable summer, the summer before my senior year at South Hagerstown High School.

## K-12: The End of the Beginning

Time flies. Here I am in my senior year of high school. It was kind of cool, as I remember, knowing that I would finally be a senior. I was reaching the apex of my less-than-illustrious but all things considered, satisfactory youth. I needed a reality check in the twelfth grade, and I think it came in the form of having friends who were excited about graduating and then moving on to college. In my mind my Commercial degree may have sounded better than a General degree, but in reality there was little difference, other than my being better at typing.

First, though, let's get through this senior year. Then I'll explore my options. At the very least, I was a little more serious about my academic pursuits in my senior year. I give credit to Miss Noll, my eleventh-grade English teacher, for making me see that there are interesting things to be learned in school beyond being a goof-off and accomplishing consistent pick-and-roll moves on the basketball court. Fortunately, I had another English teacher in my senior year, Mr. Joe Robeson, who saw some potential in me as a student. I began to take pride in that. Mr. Robeson, as you may recall if you've suffered through this tedious autobiography, was my junior varsity basketball coach. His ability to be an excellent teacher was his willingness to allow students to be themselves and express themselves, as long as it was not a distraction to the process. Occasionally he would agree with a point I was making in his English class and compliment me on my contribution, and if I made a sarcastic comment that wasn't necessarily appropriate to the conversation but not too out of line, he'd laugh with the class and we'd move on.

I'm not sure how W.B. Yeats came into the picture, but "Dooney Rock" was the topic in class, and as hard as Mr. Robeson tried to explain the significance, the more my comments got the best of him. Ultimately, he signed my senior yearbook, "To George Mikan: I hope you find your Dooney Rock." Mr. Robeson saw potential in me and that was enough to imagine my life beyond high school.

In terms of my high school basketball career, my senior year was only slightly better than my junior year. Nick Scallion was my varsity coach.

He scared me and as a result I was always nervous during games. I wouldn't say his coaching methods bordered on abuse but in my mind, they did and I knew if I made a mistake that I would face the wrath of his verbal abuse. Players react differently to different coaching methods. Some players are able to dismiss verbal abuse. I was not one of those players. I shouldn't be so hard on coach Nick Scallion. In addition to his being in the Marine Corps after college, he had been a small college All-American at Washington College in Chestertown, MD. He had a passion for basketball and for coaching. His ability to treat all of his players the same and his expectations that his players play to perfection were admirable, but were my undoing. I know I could have been a much better player with a different coach at the helm, but c'est la vie.

## Tip a Canoe and Naugle, Zook and Gabriel Too

Towards the end of my senior year of high school, Dave Zook and Jeff Gabriel, a Halfway friend, were hanging out doing nothing, and the subject of the canoe that we had in my backyard came up. Jack had rebuilt this canoe almost from scratch. It had been a wood-frame canoe and probably at one time had a canvas-type outer shell. The canoe was nothing more than a skeleton of a boat when Jack got it. Jack and his friend from the railroad actually soaked and bent the missing bow joints that went inside this boat. It was an 18' canoe, which was uncommon. Instead of rebuilding its outer shell in its original form, Jack and his friend fiber-glassed the exterior, making it really durable but incredibly heavy. To me, the finished product was a remarkable piece of workmanship, of which Jack was justifiably proud.

It occurred to us that it would be kind of cool if we could paddle Jack's canoe across the City Park Lake in Hagerstown. We determined that such a crossing had never been successfully done and we would be the first. The Hagerstown City Park was established in 1916. It's a beautiful urban park with a five-acre lake. We were convinced that since the park was opened, no one had ever taken a boat out on the lake. There were no signs that said "No Boats Allowed," and yet there was some unwritten code of boating etiquette that no one dared to test the waters with any type of flotation device. Wouldn't it be something if we could paddle this giant canoe across that lake? We would make history. People would tell stories for generations of this unprecedented voyage from the Virginia Avenue side of the lake to the shores of the Washington County Fine Arts Museum on the other side of this vast body of water that stretched 150 yards from shore to shore. In this adventurous moment of exhilaration at the thought of being a part history, the three of us carried the canoe to Gabriel's car. We put blankets on the roof of the car to protect scratching of either the car roof, which was already a rusty mess, or the canoe. We then mounted the massive canoe on the car roof and began to tie it down with ropes by looping the ropes over the top of the canoe and weaving them through open car windows and finally tying the ropes in a series of navigational knots designed to hold the canoe snugly to the roof of the car.

We pulled out of my family driveway in preparation for our upcoming voyage. Columbus would have been proud. Ten minutes later we arrived at our launch point on Virginia Avenue, coincidentally across the street from where Zook lived. We got out of the car, scanned the horizon for any signs of a police presence and were satisfied that we were safe to proceed with our plan. Quickly and carefully, we unloaded the canoe so as not to draw any attention to ourselves. We had to carry the canoe through a hedge that bordered the park and then down to the awaiting lake. Our paddles were ready. As I recall, since Gabriel was the youngest of the three of us in seniority, he sat in the middle and acted as a coxswain. Zook took the bow, and I handled the stern end of the vessel.

We eased the canoe into the water with Zook already in place in the front. Gabriel exuded good balance as he also entered the boat and made his way to the middle, and I stepped into the rear of the canoe, and with a gentle push of my left foot we entered the lake and were off. We paddled like crazy, thinking the police were surely on their way to arrest us and throw us in jail for years for daring to pull off such a stunt. It probably took us about three minutes to navigate this treacherous body of water. We arrived at the far shore, sweating like pigs. Zook jumped out in the water, which was about two feet deep, and pulled the boat to safety. Gabriel and I stepped gingerly from the canoe to the bank of the lake.

Collectively we pulled our canoe out of the water, carried it up a hill close to the museum and hid it in a way that would give us time for Gabriel to run back around the lake, get his car and bring it to our camouflaged location. Gabriel arrived five minutes later. We again checked the area for law enforcement officers lurking in the bushes, and seeing none, we loaded the canoe back on to the top of the car, tied it down and giddily rode off towards my home, thinking that we had made our mark in the history of Hagerstown antics. What a bunch of dumb asses we were—well, Zook and Gabriel were.

## Hagerstown Junior College:
## The Harvard of the South

My senior year was winding down and I needed to explore my options. I had three: 1. join the army or get drafted; 2. try to find gainful employment as a secretary; or 3. apply for and be accepted to Hagerstown Junior College. I chose door number 3.

HJC was about as good a fit as there could be for an aspiring basketball player like me. I had not yet faced the reality that it was very unlikely that I would ever play for the Boston Celtics, or for the minor league Hoboken Zephyrs for that matter, but dreams die hard. I was about as ready as most high school graduates who didn't have a clue about their future and who were ill-prepared academically for college, but

I knew that even a two-year degree would give me an advantage, a heads-up in the job market. I have to give some props to students who attended HJC simply because they couldn't afford a four-year college. There were students at HJC who were brilliant and not only went on to prestigious four-year universities but really were even smarter than their academically-gifted classmates who attended four-year colleges in that they saved a boatload of money in those first two years. Maybe HJC was indeed the Harvard of the South (south end of Hagerstown).

In terms of academics, I did enough to stay eligible to play basketball. I did okay in writing-related courses or subjects requiring a creative imagination, but in the rest of my courses my goal was simply to pass, not to learn. A "D" was perfectly acceptable as long as it was balanced with a "B" in some for-credit elective.

The first year of junior college remains the best year of competitive basketball that I've had in my extended career. I played with some really good players who were a year older than me, players who actually went to other colleges the previous year on basketball scholarships and either couldn't make it academically or got homesick: George Miles, Junior Rudy (South High), Dave Titlow (North High), Tim Lamp (Martinsburg) and another player my age, Mike Parker from somewhere in the Lancaster area of Pennsylvania. We averaged 101 points a game, but we allowed 99 points. It was so much fun.

Irv Easterday was our coach. Irv at that time was probably in his late 30's. He was the first athletic director for a community college in the state of Maryland. He was a graduate of Springfield College in Massachusetts, a physical education college affiliated with the YMCA. My brother Skip claims to have been offered a basketball scholarship to Springfield. I'm skeptical but nonetheless I'll have to take him at his word.

Irv was my kind of coach. He recognized the talent that he had on the team and pretty much let everyone have free rein on the court. I had two games that stick in my mind that were a big deal. In one game I had 24 points and 15 rebounds in a win, and my picture and article were featured in *The Morning Herald*. In another game I scored 21 points against Fort Union Military Academy. The game was held on our home court at South Hagerstown High School, and Nick Scallion was in the stands. In the second half of that game, I got a defensive rebound, dribbled the length of the court and dunked the ball. Dunking then was still an unusual occurrence. This dunk was also legitimate. It was one of those thunderous kinds of dunks. There was a great crowd there that night. Because the team was so good, we had developed a strong local following. They went nuts. As I moved back down the court, I remember pointing to Nick Scallion and taunting him. Now that was an immature thing to do for sure, and after the game I admit I felt a bit ashamed, but two nights prior to that game I scored 2 points against the South High varsity team in a South High alumni game which the alumni won. Now the South High team in 1966 was undefeated when we played them, so I understand that Nick was upset. I didn't say anything to Nick after the game. I mean, I scored 2 points. It's not like I took down his team, and aside from that he always preached that "If you play your mother one-on-one, you play to beat her.

A new Hagerstown Junior College campus had been completed for my second year at HJC. That was a big deal. It was (and is) located on Robinwood Drive in the northeast part of Hagerstown. It was a real college campus. I felt like I had arrived. I met a lot of new students from the surrounding region that year and that was kind of cool. I was expanding my circle of friends. I had passed enough courses to maintain my basketball eligibility, which of course is why I went to college. We had our own gym. In the ensuing decades a field house was built at HJC that to this day is a very impressive facility, but the new gym available to us then was a really special building.

Dave Zook and I wandered into the gym prior to the start of the first semester of classes. We spotted a couple of basketballs lying in a corner and of course felt obligated to pick them up and start shoot-ing. We got to thinking who may have been the first person to shoot hoops in the gym. One thing led to another and we decided to be the first people in the history of the new school (and perhaps in HJC his-tory) to drop-kick a basketball from half-court into the newly mounted basketball standards at both ends of the court. We proceeded in our quest. I'm pretty sure that I was the first person to successfully put a ball in the hoop from my kicking position on the half-court line. I'm sure that Zook would say that he was the first, but I would expect as much from him. I was the first. Believe me. This most assuredly is a random couple of paragraphs, but nonetheless we took personal pride in this accomplishment, regardless of it not being reported in *The Morning Herald* newspaper.

My second year of basketball was not as successful as the first from a team standpoint, but I enjoyed the experience. Irv Easterday retired and was replaced by a young coach, Bob Holup, a graduate of Bowling Green University in Ohio. I remember very little about Coach Holup. As I recall, he didn't seem like a basketball guy. He may have been a good coach but I just remember that he was there. None-the-less, we had a very competitive team. In addition to a few carry-over players from the first year, we added Tom Stough, Eddie Kipe and Gary Rice from North Hagerstown High School and Nick Fell from St. Maria Goretti and a few others from the surrounding region. In those days junior colleges were pretty much dependent on local talent, players who for various reasons remained in the area to squeeze a little more basketball out of their systems before calling it a day and moving on with their lives. I was still in denial mode. Nick Fell died of undeter-mined causes a year or two after I left HJC. Nick was not a skilled player but he was gritty and had a heart of gold. Sometimes people you meet in life, even for a brief time remain etched in your memory. Nick is one of those people.

I didn't graduate from HJC at the conclusion of my second year. When I went to the University of Baltimore, I took some courses that I needed to complete my Associate's Degree and had them transferred back to HJC to fulfil my degree requirements. I can't remember how I discovered the University of Baltimore, but I did, and I wrote a letter to their coach Paul Baker, telling him of what a find I would be for his program. He responded and invited me to an open gym try-out at Mt. St. Joseph High School in Baltimore during the summer of 1967. I don't know how I connected with George Miles, a former South High player as well as being a starter on the HJC team during my first year there. George was an excellent player. He could have played ball at a four-year school and may have started out at such a school, but either for personal reasons or maybe academics, he came back to Hagerstown. George asked me about this try-out, and he too received an invitation to come to Baltimore. I thought we both played well; however, we were not offered scholarships, and George never pursued becoming a U. of B. "Bee." I, on the other hand, was thrilled that I could be a walk-on, and fortunately my parents were willing to support my dream financially. In the fall of 1967, I was off to "Charm City."

*SUMMER*

1967-1978

## Leaving Hagerstown

In the latter part of the summer of 1967, Dave Zook, Buddy Knapp and I moved to Baltimore to attend the University of Baltimore. We pretty much decided to go there because they accepted our transcripts (mine with an astounding 1.999 GPA) from what was then Hagerstown Junior College and because the name "University" had a certain prestigious sound to it that rang our collective bells.

The University of Baltimore was a commuter school. It was founded in 1925 and was most noted as a business and law school. Most of its students came from traditional old Baltimore neighborhoods. They were children of first- and second- generation Italians, Germans, Irish and Polish with a smattering of Lithuanians thrown into the mix for good measure.

How Naugle, Zook and Knapp fit into this ethnic melting pot is beyond me, but we assimilated as best we could. We rented an apartment at the Mount Royal Apartments. This was a massive old building that had been constructed at the turn of the 20th century. Our building was one block from U. of B. The school was not what one would expect of a college campus. The main building on North Charles and Mt. Royal could easily have been mistaken for a large shoe factory. There was another large building on Howard Street about six blocks away that housed the law school as well as business classrooms. The one new building that actually resembled a college building was the Langsdale Library on Maryland Avenue, and the school's athletic facilities were located about three miles away in Mt. Washington off Northern Parkway. The athletic complex consisted of a baseball field, a soccer and lacrosse field and "band-box" of a gym. The whole complex originally was St. Paul's Boys School prior to their re-location to a beautiful campus in Baltimore County.

Our apartment cost $135.00 a month each, which our respective parents agreed to pay. It was a great apartment. Other basketball players who had been recruited to play for the "Bees" also lived there. Our two years there provided all of us with a lot of fun experiences. The three of us were enrolled in the Business Management program. I think Knapp may have been the best student among us. Zook was smart but was incredibly lazy. I was not so smart but did what I had to do to maintain grades that were good enough to keep playing basketball. I would drive each day in my Volkswagen Bug (one of three that I owned in my lifetime) to the "Bees' Nest" for practices and games. This gym was an embarrassment at best. Fortunately, it did have a college-size court, but the seating capacity for spectators was about 300 (including standing room only) and the bleachers were tight against the court. You had to go down a long set of wooden stairs to the locker room. The home locker room had mounted hangers for clothes and one 15' X 15' communal shower with three shower heads. There were three toilet stalls. The visiting locker room had a smaller area shower with one shower head and one toilet stall. Other teams coming into our building were astonished at the condition of the gym and the complete lack of amenities, amenities that any public high school would've had in Baltimore City. The Bees were in the Mason-Dixon Conference, in which there were name schools like American University, Old Dominion University and Loyola of Baltimore, all of which had proper college facilities for that era.

I was strictly a limited reserve on the teams during the two years I was there. As Zook aptly put it, I was one of those players who had red knees from propping my elbows on my knees as watched the other players, play. There were no personal highlights. In my second year (my senior year), we played LaSalle University at the Palestra in Philadelphia as part of a double-header. LaSalle was the number two-ranked basketball team in the country. The players we had on our team from Philadelphia were beside themselves. It was an opportunity to play in front of their families, and more importantly they would have a chance to play at the Palestra, which to this day is like the Holy Grail of historic basketball arenas in the United States. There also would be 8,000 people in attendance. I was in awe of the whole experience. We were beaten 103 to 54, and our Philly players were devastated. I played the last 1 minute and 14 seconds of the game, and for me it was like hitting that grand slam home run that you read about earlier in this dissertation. I played at the Palestra—something to write about—which I just did.

The experience of being a U. of B. student athlete was not lost on me—except for the student part. Being part of that basketball team enabled me to expand my horizons. We had many bus trips to different cities on the east coast. The athletic budget was always a problem. I remember taking a trip with our school's wrestling team to a game against Fairleigh Dickenson in New Jersey. The wrestlers spat in cups the entire trip in preparation for weigh-ins at the match to ensure that they made their weight class. I never understood why anyone would enjoy wrestling. That's not to say that I didn't appreciate the skill and effort it took to be a wrestler. It was just not a sport that appealed to me and my guess is the wrestlers felt the same indifference towards the game of basketball. On that trip though, we were all "Bees."

The one special trip that I remember was flying to Buffalo, New York to play the University of Buffalo. It was the first time that I ever flew. I don't know if it was an expense issue but we flew on a prop passenger plane as opposed to a jet. Since I'd never flown, I wouldn't have known the difference. I do remember distinctly though, as we ascended after take-off the plane seemed to struggle to get to the point before we actually leveled-off. It was like sitting in a reclining chair and you were kind of struggling to get the chair back to an upright sitting position. It was only later in life after flying on jets that I realized the unusualness of that first plane ride.

My academic "maintenance" plan worked relatively well during my first two years at U. of B. If I had a creative-type business class like marketing or advertising, I did okay. I could come up with creative ads and jingles that seemed to be satisfactory to the instructor in that particular class. Other classes were difficult to comprehend, and I had to be creative.

Dr. Deutsch was probably as responsible for my ultimately graduating because of the "D" I received in a statistics class in 1972 (seven years after I started college) that required a fair amount of cheating, which of course I feel bad about, but seriously, what were my options? It was statistics!

All of the athletes at U. of B. were keenly aware of another instructor's classes, those of Pop Warner. He had a PhD from Columbia University. He taught business classes, and I have no doubt that he was a brilliant man. At the time we were there, I guess Pop was in his late 60's or early 70's. He knew his subjects. My sense is that it was up to you to benefit from what he was teaching, but if you didn't, it didn't bother him. It was on you. Because of his grading system, all of his classes were hard to get into and all were overflowing.

Pop's tests were all multiple choice: "Choose A, B, C or D." Felix Bucci, a Baltimore City Little Italy resident and member of our basketball team, would volunteer to grade Pop's tests along with other volunteer athletes from the other sports teams. When taking your test you would put your name on the test paper, but you could leave the answers blank if you chose. All the papers would be collected by the volunteer graders, and Pop would begin the grading process by announcing, "The answer to question 1 is B," and the volunteer graders including Felix who was looking out for the basketball team would put "B" on your paper, and at the end of the day most athletes got an "A" or a "B." The only students who got a "C" were generally students who unfortunately were unfamiliar with the grading system. I always thought that Pop must have received some special dispensation or under-the-table payments from U. of B.'s athletics department.

I had a great two years at U. of B (well, actually five years, counting the three years of taking part-time classes beyond my basketball years). I met a lot of interesting people from many different places and backgrounds. I began to assimilate into the culture of Baltimore City and to understand the dynamics of the influence of economic opportunities and lack thereof in different parts of the city which were dominated by African-Americans. I took trips to cities on the east coast that I would probably have never visited if not for having the opportunity to play basketball. As a result of playing for the University of Baltimore Bees, I made contacts which ultimately led to my career, and I became friends with my teammates, whose friendships I fondly remember. All of my teammates during those two years went on to have successful careers and families. Isaiah "Bunny" Wilson, the only Black player on my team in my senior year, went on to play two years in the N.B.A. for the Detroit Pistons. I lived my professional basketball career vicariously through Bunny. Robert Borski, a point guard from Philadelphia, became a four-term U.S. Congressman from Pennsylvania. I went on to be the Director of Therapeutic Recreation for the Baltimore City Department of Recreation and Parks.

## Taking a Road Less Traveled (or Not Even Known about)

Despite my professional aspirations being squashed, basketball has always benefited me. At the end of the '69 season, Roger Gaeckler, an assistant basketball coach at U. of B., told me about a job that he had as aquatics director at the Baltimore League for Crippled Children and Adults. (That name ultimately became The League for People with Disabilities, which was much more acceptable to all concerned.) Roger was leaving this job and his job as an assistant coach to accept a head coach job at Lebanon Valley College in Annville, Pennsylvania. Roger, who for some reason took a shine to me, asked me if I was interested, brought me to the site and introduced me to some of people with disabilities whom he worked with, and then said, "Do you want the job?" I was in year four of college with no job, no degree and not much chance of finding or attaining either, so I took the job, and up to that point it was the best decision that I had ever made. My parents made a financial sacrifice for me to attend U. of B. I was appreciative of their sacrifice then and told them that I would finish my degree, which as you read on you will see that I indeed did.

## The League

So, in 1969 I began what would become a career in therapeutic recreation at what was then the League for Crippled Children and Adults in Baltimore City. Advocates for people with disabilities were later responsible for changing the name to The League for People with Disabilities. The League was (and still is) a private out-patient rehabilitation center, whose services then included physical therapy, occupational therapy, a workshop for adults with disabilities and a therapeutic recreation department where I became the adapted aquatics director. I was also a support staff person to Ralph Smith, the Director of Camping and Recreation. My job included being involved with all of the social programs for both children and adults with disabilities. That included Friday night dances, wheelchair square-dancing, special trips for adults, Saturday swim classes and parties for kids with disabilities.

In 1970 my supervisor Ralph Smith founded the Baltimore Ravens wheelchair basketball team. It was the first wheelchair basketball program in Maryland and has remained an entity through current times. The Baltimore Ravens are now the Maryland Ravens to differentiate themselves from the Baltimore Ravens Football Team. Because of my extensive and "distinguished" basketball career, Ralph asked me if I would like to coach this new team. I knew nothing about wheelchair basketball but the position was certainly in keeping with my experience as an adapted aquatics director. I was the head coach for two years. We may have won three games. The players that we began that program with formed the core group of players who went on to have great success. I have kept in touch with many of these players over the years and they remain good friends. When I do run into them, they'll recall those early games when we would lose 105 to 33. We can all laugh about those games...now.

In 1971 Ralph found a job in Baltimore for Tom Brown, a recent graduate of the University of Illinois. Tom was a nationally known top-flight wheelchair basketball player. There are always arguments in all sports whether or not a great player from a previous era could be as good in the current era. Tom Brown is one of those players who could have made that transition. He was the best chair-handler that I had ever seen, and he could score easily from any part of the court. In 1974 he took a team of local players with disabilities to the National Wheelchair Basketball Tournament and the team finished in 3rd place, which was an amazing accomplishment.

One of the team's best players from Baltimore was Tony Hewitt, a fourteen-year-old player who had been shot two years prior by an errant bullet that hit him while he was riding his bike in East Baltimore. This injury left him with permanent spinal cord damage that limited his ability to walk except with crutches. Tony remains an example of what sports can do for someone, along with having a support system of family and friends to provide an avenue for a successful life. Tony became an excellent player, but more importantly he saw the potential he had in life off the court. He had mentors and my future wife Cass and I were among those who encouraged him to get through high school and go on to college. Tony finished college, spent several years as a missionary in French Guiana, came home, found his future wife

Teresa, got married and has had a very successful life in Queens, New York. It all started with basketball.

In addition to the aquatics program, I got involved with the League's summer residential camp, Camp Greentop, as well as all of the other adapted recreation programs throughout the week and on weekends.

Camp Greentop was founded in 1938. It is the second-oldest residential summer camp in the United States for children and adults with disabilities. It is located in the Catoctin Mountains in Thurmont, Maryland, and is about a half mile from Camp David, the Presidential retreat. The childrens' camp sessions were for many years six to seven weeks long during the summer. There have been thousands of kids who attended the Camp and had wonderful, memorable experiences, but I will focus on my years there and what they meant to me and to those campers and staff who were a part of Greentop from 1969 to 1978.

The childrens' camp enabled children with disabilities to experience the joy of just being a kid. Staff were oriented to give each camper a sense of self-worth and to offer opportunities and experiences that they otherwise would not have had, coming as they did from economically disadvantaged communities. Activities included whitewater rafting, horse-back riding, adapted sports, swimming, theater and social interactions with kids and staff from different backgrounds. The campers had experiences that their peers in the communities where they lived could only dream about. The campers' exposure to new experiences and the interactions that they had with other kids from better economic situations and with staff, some of whom came from different parts of the world, helped these campers to assimilate into the mainstream as they moved into adulthood. They had a much better understanding of people who lived in communities different from theirs. Likewise, the many staff members at Camp Greentop benefitted from knowing these kids, understanding their disabilities, being exposed to kids from different races and cultural backgrounds and learning about the communities in which they lived. Many of the staff went on to careers that involved working with people with disabilities.

I have had the honor of knowing so many of these kids when they became adults. Those whom I have kept in touch have all had successful lives. If you asked them what was the most influential thing that happened to them in their lifetime, most would say, "Camp Greentop."

The adult camp at Camp Greentop was a two-week end-of-summer camp. In the early 70's, unless you or your family were incredibly wealthy and could afford around the clock personal care, you really didn't have too many vacation options. Camp Greentop was a true vacation for many adults with disabilities. I will try not to get too carried away with the passion I felt for this program and for the campers. Like kids' camp, the adult camp provided an opportunity for two weeks of adult fun and endeavors where people were treated with dignity. Physical needs were taken care of by staff and all of programs and activities were inclusive.

It was a diverse group of campers, especially in terms of disability. There were people who would have been considered to have developmental disabilities, and we had campers who were college-educated, some of whom had been scientists, teachers and doctors, among other professions, but all had physical, developmental or emotional disabilities that were debilitating enough that would have prevented them from going on a conventional vacation without a 24-hour support staff. Camp Greentop had such a staff who worked the two-week session for $200. The staff were an empathetic collection of hippies, college students, teachers, researchers, professors and random generalists who enjoyed the opportunity to meet new people and have a good time doing so.

Our goal was to provide programs and experiences that were meaningful and adult- oriented. We had great on-site activities including less-than-extravagant but amazingly funny theatrical productions, competitive table games, political discussion groups, sports activities, crafts, swimming, sunbathing and great meals. On banquet night, held on the last night of camp, it wasn't uncommon to have a full-fledged luau with roasted pig and all of the associated fixings including "adult beverages."

The staff person who was responsible for inspiring our liberal attitudes was our Adult Camp Director, Pete Setlow. Pete, interestingly enough, is a distinguished Professor in the Department of Molecular Biology and Biophysics at the University of Connecticut, but his true calling was that of a Camp Director who provided comic relief to both staff and campers during the annual two-week summer adult camp. His job as a researcher was just a sideline that he did for the other 50 weeks of the year.

We also had a lot of out of camp trips that could include anything from a trip to the horse racing track in Charlestown, West Virginia to white water rafting on the Potomac River near Harpers Ferry. I should mention here that in the seventies, lift vans were an anomaly. Our mode of travel included cars, station wagons and passenger vans. Staff physically transferred people from their wheelchairs into whatever mode of transportation was available, fold their wheelchairs and load them into the back of the vehicle. Then the process would be reversed when we reached our destination and again for the trip back to camp. It was a physically exhausting process but the emotional high that you received from seeing people with disabilities have such a great time more than compensated for the lingering aches and pains from the transfers and loading. It was always about providing a new experience that in all probability a camper with a disability would never have had, if not for Camp Greentop.

One of the aforementioned campers was a dear friend throughout Cass' and my life, Terry Berzofsky. Terry was the same age as me. She was born with cerebral palsy. She was without a doubt one of the most physically disabled people that I've known in my life. She was totally dependent upon others for her personal care that included helping her to eat and drink which she did with great difficulty. For most of her adult life she communicated by spelling words out on a spelling board with a head stick that her brother Henry had devised, and by simply using obvious facial expressions to indicate yes and no responses or agreement or disagreement when various topics of conversation were presented to her.

Intellectually, she was brilliant. She was an insatiable reader and the knowledge that she had about all aspects of life never seized to amaze those who knew her. She had an extremely supportive family who made people aware constantly about Terry's high intellect. Beyond the League and Camp Greentop, people who knew Terry well would invite her to concerts, restaurants, camping trips, festivals and whatever event that her friends knew she would enjoy. The two weeks of Camp Greentop that Terry spent every summer of her life were the catalyst to the world beyond her wheelchair. She would take advantage of every out-of-camp trip opportunity available. One of the many trips that she ventured out on was Cunningham Falls, which is a beautiful waterfall located in Cunningham Falls State Park, not too far from camp. Getting to the top of falls involved climbing up a series of large and at times, slippery rocks. I estimate that it was about a 100-foot climb. For an able-bodied adult it's not overly difficult but it does present some challenges and climbing carefully is certainly recommended. When we asked Terry if she'd like to climb to the top, there was no hesitation on her part. She was in. Terry may have made this trek a few times in later years but I remember carrying her up on what I think was one of her first adventures to the top. Another staff person carried up Terry's folded wheelchair which was no small task. I remember finally getting to the apex of the falls, placing Terry in her wheelchair and just sitting there in amazement that we were there and had avoided tumbling down the falls to an almost certain death. All of us just sat there with smiles on our collective faces at what we accomplished. The fact that Terry trusted us to do this enhanced our courage to make the climb. Terry passed away sometime in the 2000's. In her life she probably accomplished more with less than any person I have ever known. I've talked about survivors throughout this book but if I had to rank them, Terry would be at the very top of the list.

As a footnote to this story, I think you should know how Cunningham Falls got its name. I cannot help but think that while you were reading this story about Terry that you also wondered, "How did Cunningham Falls get its name?" I feel obliged to tell you. Hundreds of years ago, before the white man lived in this area, Native Americans inhabited the region. In that time, the most important food that the Native Americans sought out was wild boar. A wild boar that was properly roasted in a wood fire pit was not only delicious and nutritious, it was believed that the animal also provided great physical strength and intelligence. As the story goes, among the many wild boar that roamed the forests, there was one boar that was not only the largest of all the boars but also the smartest. He was seen sporadically but he was incredibly evasive and always escaped capture. It was decided by the Native American tribe that capturing this super boar would make them the smartest people in all the land. They got together and plotted a plan that would enable them to finally trap and kill the boar. They knew the area where he would mostly likely be, so a large group of Native Americans came and met together in the wooded area where the boar lived. They all held hands and slowly moved on foot through the woods until miraculously they came upon the large wild boar. They knew he couldn't get past them, so they cautiously herded the boar to the top of the waterfalls where they knew there would be no escape route for this beast among beasts. Now, the wild boar was a proud boar. He realized that he was about to be captured and eaten. As he looked at his options, he realized that the only way to avoid capture and save pride was to jump off the top of falls, knowing that his death was eminent. So, as the Native Americans approached, he leaped to his death. As the Native Americans stood in wonderment, the Chief of the tribe, in his wisdom said to his fellow warriors, "Ah… cunning ham falls." Many people will groan when they read this, but Terry laughed her head off every time she heard it.

There is one other trip that sticks in my mind that was much different but provided the same result. Some staff members and I took six men in wheelchairs to a professional wrestling match at the National Guard Armory on North Potomac Street in Hagerstown. As some of you might be aware, professional wrestling, while requiring certain athletic skills, tends to be more entertainment than actual wrestling that one would see on the high school or college level. The campers in attendance on this particular evening watched their wrestling heroes on television, loved professional wrestling and were excited to see an actual match. This was a group of guys who bordered on having mild developmental disabilities as well as physical ones; however, all of them were very communicative, and I always enjoyed having conversations with them. They were also kind of shy, saying very little unless someone would work hard to engage them in a conversation.

To my absolute amazement, all of that changed when the wrestling match began. Men whom I had never heard express more than a sentence or two began screaming at the top of their lungs at the wrestlers. Their eyes were bulging, and the veins in their necks and foreheads were popping out. In crystal-clear voices they spewed out expletives at the "bad guy" wrestlers that I think even startled the wrestlers. I almost expected to see them jump out of their wheelchairs cheering for Chief Strongbow. He was a professional wrestler from that era who generally was the protagonist in the theater of professional wrestling. Everyone in attendance enjoyed the wrestling match, but I think the crowd and maybe even the wrestlers themselves enjoyed more seeing these six guys in wheelchairs having such a great time. By the time we got back to camp later that night, everyone was exhausted. The six men had lost their voices, but what a memorable evening. The good guys won.

## Hit by a Lightning Bolt

The other life-changing event that happened to me in the 1970's was that I got married. Mary Catherine Walker, aka Cass, came into my life during this time. A social worker at the League named Mary Farfel asked me what I would look for in a wife, and I responded, "A woman who is thin and smart." Mary was befuddled.

Around that time, I believe in 1971, I had completed (with the help of Ralph Smith) the last course I needed to get a B.S. Degree in Business Management from the University of Baltimore. Since it had taken seven years of my life to achieve this momentous accomplishment, I decided that I should have my picture taken for the U. of B. yearbook. The school an arrangement with the photography department at Hutzler's Department Store on Howard Street in downtown Baltimore. I went there and met this beautiful young woman who was the photographer for Hutzler's. Her name was Julie Walker. We kind of hit off, I guess because she thought as a college graduate, I had some potential (little did she know). I was so smitten that I asked her out, something that normally I would not have had the courage to do, but I was about to get my B.S. degree after all. Julie lived in the Roland Park section of Baltimore, so I figured she must've been making a really good salary. Did I say I was little naïve back in the day? We dated for a few months.

Spring had sprung and summer was now upon us. Julie had a sister, Cass, who had just graduated from Archbishop Keough High School in Baltimore, and her class were looking forward to their senior class trip to Ocean City, Maryland. Would I like to go to the ocean and give her sister Cass a lift also? Sure, a weekend at Ocean City sounded adventurous, and who knew what it might lead to? There may have been some ulterior motives involved, but certainly not on my part. The plan was in place. On a late Friday afternoon, I drove my Volkswagen to Hutzler's to meet Julie and her sister Cass. Julie waved me down and I was immediately struck by her young, thin, beautiful and incredibly smart sister.

As soon as Cass got in the back seat of my Bug I was enthralled. To make a long story as short as possible, a few months after the Ocean City trip Julie found her calling and life-partner with John Bruce Baker, a (somewhat) radical Presbyterian minister living a communal-like existence in the Hampden area of Baltimore, and sometime in the interim I asked Julie if I could ask her sister Cass out. Things moved quickly after our initial date. This is the woman that I wanted to spend the rest of my life with, and almost fifty years later, I can hardly believe that here I am recounting that amazing life with Cass.

Cass and I were married at Our Lady of Good Counsel Catholic Church, the same church she grew up in and adjacent to the same building where she went to school from the first through eighth grades. She as well as her seven other siblings (very Catholic-like) lived directly across the street from the church in a row house with three bedrooms and one bathroom, just like every other house on the block. Ralph Smith, my supervisor and sometime mentor from my job at the League, was my best man. The wedding reception was held about two blocks away at the "German Church," as it was known, or *Deutsches Vereingte Evangelisches Kirche*, its proper name.

The German Church was literally built for immigrants when they got off the boat in Locust Point in the early 20th century. An interesting thing about that church is, for as long as we lived in Locust point, which we did for over twenty years after we got married, everyone in that neighborhood referred to that church as the "Lutheran" church. It was not. It was the same denomination in which I had grown up, which was the United Church of Christ. This was a "Zwingli" parish. Ulrich

Zwingli was the founder of the Swiss Reformed Church in the 1500's. After several reincarnations it became the Evangelical and Reformed Church and ultimately the United Church of Christ. I guess because this was the church of my upbringing it all always bothered me that the "German" Church in Locust Point was referred to as the Lutheran Church. There were three churches in Locust Point, which was incidentally a peninsula that ended at Fort McHenry National Park. The other church was Episcopalian, which of course was the "Public's" version of the Catholic Church. In Locust Point you were either a "Public" (non-Catholic) or Catholic, depending on whether you went to Catholic school or public school.

In addition to the three churches in the "Point," there was at least one bar in every single block. If you wanted to drown your sorrows, you were always only steps away from drowning. I could go on and on about Locust Point. It was composed of Germans, Polish and Irish, with Germans and Poles predominating, and most older people were second or third generation immigrants. Older people who lived there were well-versed in the language from the old country from which they emigrated and English. It was not uncommon to hear a combination of German and Polish conversations. At Christmas time the German church sang carols on German, and in the Catholic church the children's choir learned to sing Polish carols phonetically.

After Cass and I were married, we lived for a very short time in Colmar Apartments, the very same complex that Zook and Knapp had lived in until 1970. Within a year, however, Cass was the recipient of a small inheritance from a distant relative, and we bought a small row house about a block away from Cass's home in Locust Point for $6,500. Cass had started at Towson College (now University) in 1970. She continued to go to school to get her degree while I continued working at the League. Cass got her Bachelor's degree in art in 1974. She was an excellent artist. Her specialty was woodworking. When she graduated, she got her first job related to her field (not really her first job; she started teaching guitar lessons in the neighborhood when she was twelve). Cass worked for Streuver Brothers Construction, an upstart company specializing in renovating row houses for their eventual "gentrification." Cass finished wood for inclusion as part of the construction.

Cass loved the work but decided to seek a job that would provide a little more stability. She applied for and was hired as an Activities Director for a Baltimore City nursing home. The facility was formerly the "James Brown Motor Inn" but had been bought and converted into a nursing home for the oddest but always interesting people who were fortunately identified by State Department of Social Services as being qualified residents. This is another one of those stories that could be turned into a book, but I only have one life to live, and I believe this book will have to serve as my legacy. Cass did an absolutely fantastic job with this group of folks, many of whom were former residents of state psychiatric institutions.

Cass then decided to improve her marketability by going back to school. She applied for and was accepted into the Morgan State University's Recreation Management Master's Program. Morgan State was a historically Black college and Cass received a minority scholarship to complete her degree, which she completed in 1976.

Cass also helped me get finish my undergraduate degree. In 1975 I was fortunate to know Ralph W. Jones, Jr., at professor at both Morgan State and the University of Baltimore. We knew one another through my providing in-service learning programs at the League for his Morgan students. Ralph initiated a Master's program in Urban Recreation at the University of Baltimore, and because of his help I got into that program, which was a career builder for me. I loved this program, but I could not have completed it without Cass's help. I received my Master's degree in 1977.

I forgot to mention that in 1975 we purchased a three-story row house a few blocks from our original purchase. The house, which was located at 1477 Reynolds Street, was owned by a cousin of Cass's. At one point in its history, it had actually been a small warehouse. We bought that house for $20,000 and lived in it until 1995. It was a great house. I have wonderful memories of the house and the neighborhood. The one striking feature of the house was that Cass's cousin, who was an amateur artist of some renown, had built a water fountain in the living room of the house, complete with a waterfall, tropical trees painted on the wall adjacent to the fountain and scantily-clad Hawaiian dancers adorning the walls. We kept the fountain intact for the twenty years that we lived there. It was quite the topic of conversation.

There were wonderful stories about Cass's family as well as the Locust Pointers who inhabited this village of German, Polish and Irish immigrants. I guess when Cass writes her autobiography, she can go into detail about her parents, but I would still like to pass along a few memories of them. Cass's parents Mary (Mare) and Charles (Char) were two of the nicest people that you'd ever want to meet or have as parents. Mare was the sweetest lady. She was the one that encouraged every one of her kids to get a good education, and she worked with all of them tirelessly in their early years to ensure they had the educational foundation that they needed to succeed in life. Cass had seven other siblings and they are all successful.

Mare was a devout Catholic, and all her kids attended the Catholic School which was located directly across the street from their home. When I say Mare was a "devout" Catholic, she was a person who practiced the "Golden Rule." She was accepting of any person who came into her home and never had a negative thing to say about anyone. She ironed the church altar cloths and made countless angel costumes and batches of cupcakes when her children volunteered her services to the nuns.

Cass's father was an amazing man. He had a fourth-grade education but had the mind of Archimedes. He was a mathematician, engineer and inventor. He also had great physical strength and could move things, lift things and adjust things that required ropes, pulleys and ingenuity that astounded his family and friends. He was a longshoreman on Baltimore's waterfront. He never made more than $7,500 a year and yet through being vigilant in saving every penny he possibly could, he was able to support his family. He did all this while suffering from chronic mental health problems his entire life. I point this out only to say that he knew what he needed to do to cope with his illness, and no matter how bad things got for him, he had a family that he loved and he did what was absolutely necessary to provide for them. He was one of the strongest men I ever knew and his perseverance was his greatest strength. One of the testaments to his physical strength and his engineering mind was a 1,000 lb. solid marble slab that he and my mother-in-law, Mare moved from somewhere in the neighborhood to our house on Fort Ave. and Reynolds Street. This was a project that they came up with on their own. Where Char discovered this solid block of marble, he decided to solicit Mare's help to move this huge marble step to our house. It was to be a surprise bench for the front of our house. He placed metal pipes under the stone and he attached some sort of harness or rope to the block of marble. He would pull the massive block on the rolling pipes. When the block passed over the pipes, Mare would collect the pipes left behind as they exit the block of marble at the bottom and she would then come to the front of the marble and put them at the front and Char would again pull the marble on the new set of pipes and the process would continue like this, four or five feet at a time until they reached our house. We didn't see them do this. It would have had to take several hours to make this monumental trek. When the marble monument to perseverance, ingenuity and strength was finally in place, Mare said to Char. "Char, I have blisters on my hands". In response, Char said to Mare, "Mare, you should've worn gloves." Needless to say, when we arrived home and saw this new concrete monument of a bench sitting next to our steps at the back of our house, we were astounded. The block of marble became a focal point in the community and a group of older men from our street regularly gathered there to listen to the ball game together.

Char was a survivor. If there was a penny to be saved, a can or piece of metal to be salvaged and sold, whatever it took, Char did what was necessary to make sure he could support his family. I remember that a family in the neighborhood had a new sidewalk pad put down in front of their house, and someone stuck a quarter in the concrete, which hardened around the shiny piece of metal. Char happened to be walking up the street a couple of days later after the concrete had set. He noticed the quarter embedded in the sidewalk and without hesitation pulled out a pocket knife, dug out the quarter, stuck it in his pocket and continued with his walk.

When Char worked on the waterfront, sometimes goods on the ships which were meant for delivery to customers "accidentally" found their way off the ship under questionable circumstances and were delivered to unintended customers. Likewise, some of the men put "dummy" relatives on the payroll and collected their salaries in addition to their own. Char was appalled by this practice. Besides being the hardest-working man on the waterfront, he was unquestionably the most honest.

To supplement his income, Char had a license to collect junk on the side, and he also collected metals such as copper, tin and brass to be reimbursed by the pound for it. He had heard about an old tug that sunk, and he was determined to obtain the copper and brass fittings on the boat which was under about twelve feet of water. Char and his buddy Fritz came up with a salvage plan. Char got a metal bucket and bicycle pump that he rigged with a long garden hose in place of the small hose that was used to pump bike tires. The metal pail was rigged to be used as a sort of diver's helmet.

They must have borrowed a small boat which they anchored above the sunken tug.

Char and Fritz hung up a rope ladder that they lowered into the water where boat was. Char gingerly lowered himself into the water on the rope, all the while wearing this diving bucket over his head and with a hose in his mouth. He slowly descended into the water to dislodge the brass fittings on the tug. It was Fritz's job to pump air through the hose that Char had in his mouth by using the bike pump, which enabled Char to breathe under the water with this bucket helmet on his head. When Char filled a container with the metal fittings, he tugged on the rope ladder, and Fritz helped pull him to the surface with his bounty in hand. They were pleased with their success.

About the fourth or fifth time back down in the water, however, things went awry. Char stopped getting air through the hose, began to panic and pulled on the rope ladder for Fritz to pull him up but got no response. Knowing that drowning was imminent, he somehow managed to climb up the rope ladder, and choking and sputtering, made it safely to the deck of the ship. Fritz was not at the pump. Then he saw Fritz standing on the deck said, "Fritz—what the hell's wrong with you? Why did you stop pumping air to me?" Fritz took a quick puff of his cigarette and responded, "Sorry, Charlie, I had to take a smoke break." I swear this is a true story.

## Polish Wisdom

Locust Point was such a close community. Everybody knew everybody else, and if you grew up in Locust Point you were part of a family. People from outside of the neighborhood were not necessarily viewed with suspicion, but you sensed that the residents knew you were not a Locust Pointer. You were treated politely. Even if you moved there and lived there for a long time, which I had done, you were not quite a full-fledged member of the neighborhood. I took pride in being viewed as a transplanted and accepted member, but part of that acceptance was because I was married to a Locust Pointer. I would compare it to a Christian who decides to convert to Judaism. You were accepted by the community, but yet there was always an asterisk beside your name, as if to say "He's not a real Locust Pointer, but we appreciate his efforts."

Cass' sister Trish had worked as a nurse at Camp Greentop in the 70's and 80's, and she met many people from Baltimore City who had disabilities. Trish and Cass befriended a lot of these people, and they became part of her year-round social network. One such friend was MacArthur Crawford (Mac). Mac was a young African-American man who had muscular dystrophy. Mac was a good-looking guy, very smart and with a great sense of humor. He needed a wheelchair to get around.

One Saturday afternoon, sometime in the 70's, Trish picked up Mac at his home. Mac had three brothers and a sister who also coped with muscular dystrophy. Once Trish picked Mac up, their destination was Trish's home, her parent's house in Locust Point. Trish had some other friends with her. They all helped get Mac out of the car, up the front steps and into the rowhouse. Trish's mother Mare greeted Mac like she would greet anyone coming into her house. She welcomed him and told him he was always welcome to visit. It was a nice day and Trish decided to move the party to the backyard, which was a 10' X 10' concrete slab bordering the back alley. They got Mac down the back steps to the "patio" and were sitting there having drinks and snacks when the next-door neighbor Mrs. Novak looked out of her back door and saw Mac sitting on the Walkers' patio.

Mac was definitely not from Locust Point, and Mrs. Novak was curious. She looked over the fence separating her concrete yard from her neighbors' concrete yard, and Trish introduced Mac to Ms. Novak. She greeted him and then asked in her Locust Point (but decidedly

Polish) accent, "What's wrong witcha?" and Mac smiled and said, "I have "muscular dystrophy," at which point Mrs. Novak responded, "It's always somethin' ain't it." I guess with that affirmation Mac became a Locust Pointer.

## Achieving Random Goals, Randomly

One of my "basketball" goals in life was to live in a community where there was a basketball court next to my house. I achieved that goal. The Locust Point Recreation Center was diagonal from our rowhouse. In addition to the center, there was Latrobe Park, a great little community park which served our kids well in future years, and there were two large basketball courts with lights. For the twenty years we lived there, I played pick-up basketball there two or three nights a week. My brother-in-law, Matt honed his skills on that court. He turned out to be one of the best players in the "Point." My friend Will Kohlhoff was another regular. Will's skill set was a little different than Matt's. While he was decent player, whatever shortfalls he may have had, he made up for in intensity. Somewhere along the line some coach told him that if you wanted to win games, you had to dive for the ball if necessary. We also played ball in an area of Baltimore called "Pigtown" in an old church building that had a gym that was about 60' long and 40' wide. There were literally no out of bounds. If the ball hit the wall, it was out-of-bounds. Players were stunned from time to time to see Will slamming up against the wall in an attempt to keep the ball in play for his team. We'd go out for beers after the games, and invariably Will was a major topic of conversation. Will was a soccer goalie in college. His diving experience must've have come from that. If he missed a ball, it surely wasn't for the lack of trying. He has remained a friend of our family for almost 50 years and he still lives in Locust Point; well, he was born there but he now lives "up the hill." Anyone growing up in Locust Point were Locust Pointers but anyone growing up or moving beyond Lawrence Street, lives "up the hill."

One last athletic achievement that I associate with this time is completing my one and only marathon. Running events started to come into vogue during these years, and I started running short 5-K events on weekends in and around Baltimore. The Maryland Marathon was my goal. It was a much-publicized event, and I began to train for it on my own terms, not having a clue as to how to train properly. I trained on the sidewalks of South Baltimore and on the loop around Fort McHenry. I had no idea what I was doing but I figured running five or six miles every day would prepare me. My goal was to finish the Maryland Marathon in under four hours. My finishing time as I limped across the finish line was three hours and forty-six minutes. I included this story just to show that I was more than just a basketball player. I was not just a one-trick pony.

*Five-year old Mike with his pugnacious "Pug"*
*in front of the invisible apple tree.*

*The Roessner Ave. house in which I grew up.*

*My Mom, Hazel, My Dad, Jack, and Joyce Conrad and me on a picnic table at Cowan's Gap State Park, a week-end and summer vacation family destination for many years.*

*Me, Billy Fridinger and Jimmy Scott in front of "The Eagles Club."*

*Mom, Hazel, as a young woman in Chambersburg, Pennsylvania*

*Father, Jack, as a young soldier at the beginning of World War II.*

*Naugle Family Christmas on Roessner Ave. Left to right Me, Jack,
Hazel and my brother Skip*

*Me at Cowan's Gap paddling the canoe that was refurbished by Jack and later used to cross the mighty City Park Lake in Hagerstown, Maryland*

*Hartle's Sub Shop, a daily destination of mine during my junior high school years. Hartle's "hot" Italian cold-cut is arguably the best in the world.*

*Naugle family at the Luxemburg Gardens in Paris, France in 2008. Left to right son Michael, Daughter Kate, wife Cass, Mike and daughter Emma. It was this or Disney World. We chose Paris.*

*Farring-BayBrook Recreation Center – Pictured are the many Camp Variety campers and staff (me to the left) posing on the best adapted playground in Baltimore City. Camp Variety is a very memorable part of my life as it is for the campers and staff who each summer for the twenty years that I worked there.*

Junior League Basketball Team. This is me on the bottom row (#23 just like Michael Jordan). This team was my introduction to competitive basketball.

South Hagerstown High School Basketball Team, 1965. I am on the top row #52 next to Coach Nick Scallion.

This is my *Hagerstown Junior College* second year team. I am
number 52. Players of note are number 42, Tom Stough, my former
*Regal Fence* colleague and Dave Zook, number 44 and Jeff Gabriel,
number 32, my subordinates on the great *City Park Lake* crossing,
a memory that is only etched in our minds.

MIKE NAUGLE
U. OF BALTIMORE

*University of Baltimore – My two years at the University of Baltimore were not successful playing-wise but they were two really fun years of basketball.*

*Coach of Baltimore Ravens – I was the first coach of the Baltimore Ravens wheelchair basketball team in 1970. I remember these players fondly.*

*Coach of the Baltimore Wheelchair Athletic Club – In the 1980's I coached the Baltimore Wheelchair Athletic Club (BWAC) which at the time was sponsored by Abbey Medical. This was another group of players who meant a lot to me.*

*Coach of the high school team in the Championnat Scolaire in Zinder, Niger while in the Peace Corps. This team won the Nigerien High School Championship. This was an inspiring group of young men.*

*Basketball team in the Maryland Senior Olympics –
Even with a hip replacement I've continued to play basketball,
"play" being a relative term.*

*Naugle on stationary bike after completing 2 tours around world, raising funds for the Alzheimer's Association. As I ride off into the sunset pushing 75 years old, I will be continuing my quest to reach the moon.*

## FALL
## 1978-2007

## A New Era Begins

1978 was a pivotal year. I had been the Camping and Recreation Director for a couple of years. The long hours and the pressures associated with directing the program had taken a physical and mental toll on me. For reasons I cannot explain, I had thought about the Peace Corps in my younger years, and Africa always kind of intrigued me. Cass too was looking for some kind of career change. We talked about joining the Peace Corps, and I secretly hoped she would say, "We're too old for that," but to my surprise, she was on board with the idea, and I could not back down at that point. We still had our beloved Reynolds Street home, and we rented our house to Cass's sister Trish and her husband Bob. We completed the vetting process with Peace Corps America, filled out all of the paperwork, were accepted and were ready to set off on an adventure.

I should mention also that when we joined the Peace Corps, I was thirty-two years old and Cass was twenty-seven. We found out later that there were people older than we were who signed for the Corps de la Paix, but the group of volunteers who were among our cohort were for the most part just out of college. As time went on, we became known as "Mom" and "Dad."

It is very difficult to describe our Peace Corps experience in a way that would do it justice. In retrospect it was the best decision that we made in our lives, but believe me, in the beginning there were many days where we were questioning our decision. We left the United States from Washington, D.C., in January, 1979. Our first stop was Paris. Neither Cass nor I had ever been on a trans-Atlantic flight. The ten-hour flight in a really cramped environment should have been enough for us to ask for a return ticket home, but we persevered. I remember that the temperature in D.C. on the day of our departure was about 20 degrees, which was somewhat comparable when we landed in Paris, but I can't be sure because we had to stay on the plane. The "City of Lights" would have to remain dark until our return trip two-and-a-half years later.

Our destination was Ouagadougou, Upper Volta, a city and country that I had never heard of in my life. Like everything I've ever done, I did little research into Upper Volta or the country to which we were assigned, Chad. I guess our time in the air from D.C. to Ouagadougou was about twenty hours. We were coming from not only freezing temperatures but also from another world and another time to some extent.

We landed in Niamey, Niger, West Africa, around noon on a date that remains hidden in the archives of time travel, but sometime in February of 1979. Niamey, the capital city of Niger, was our last stopover before completing the journey to Ouagadougou. When we arrived in Niamey, we were told that we could exit the plane, but we would have to stay together as a group and stay in the terminal. When the plane door opened and we were able to head down the steps to the tarmac, the heat from the outdoors was the most intense hot air I've ever experienced. Combined with the brilliant sunlight that threatened to blind us it was as if we had landed on the sun. It was at least 115 degrees on the blistering tarmac once we descended the stairs of the plane. Collectively we sought shelter in the open-air terminal until we received word to reboard the D.C. for the final 500-mile flight to Ouagadougou.

We arrived in "Ouaga" in the early evening and stayed at the Peace Corps hostel there. The next day our new reality began in earnest. The vaccinations required to travel and live in West Africa are as follows: hepatitis A and B, typhoid, cholera, yellow fever, rabies, anthrax and meningitis. I remember that we all got the bulk of these shots when we woke up the next morning. The Peace Corps staff prepared the last of what we would remember as an American breakfast. While we appreciated the food, the after-effects of the shots, the dull aches and the incredible tiredness related to jet lag had taken a toll.

Ouagadougou is a colonial French city of about one million people, depending on who you talk to. There were some modern buildings, mostly European chain hotels, but most of the city is a hodge-podge of older buildings built from whatever the material of the day may have included. There were also remnants of the homes of French expatriates. There were parks and museums, but they were in run-down shape. Basic survival was the objective of *Les Voltaiques.* Upper Volta became Burkina Faso in 1984. I just Googled the new proper term for the people, and they are known as "Burkinabe." Back to business.

We were told that we should explore the city after breakfast on that first full day in the country. As we moved towards center city there were beggars everywhere, and there was a constant barrage of "Donne moi un cadeau" ("Give me a gift") from what seemed like every inhabitant of the city. People, both children and adults, were literally hanging onto our pants legs. Poverty was pervasive, but the human condition of these people didn't do poverty justice. It was so hot and so miserable. Had we imagined what a poor country would be like when we were still in the States, we imagined wrongly. It was during this time that Cass and I both thought about our circumstances, our future and our ability to stay there. The one thing that affected me most was that it was February of 1979. We would not only miss the Christmas of 1979 but also the Christmas of 1980. It was going to be an eternity.

Thank God there were bars in Ouagadougou. We were given enough of a stipend to eat and drink for that day. We somehow found our way to a local bar. I had no French language skills, but fortunately beer is "bier" in French, so for a short time with hid ourselves away in this bar with no air-conditioning, but it did have overhead fans that stirred the air. After consuming a "bier" or deux, nature called. The one bathroom was a unisex (not by design but by necessity), and it had metal foot pads that you either stood on to pee or, if you were of the opposite sexual persuasion, squat on. Now, that would've been acceptable except there was also water of suspect origin that slightly covered the metal foot pads that you stood or squatted on. There were no options. You waded in, peed and sloshed back out into the bar. As much as those vaccine shots hurt and made us ache, I was grateful for them because they were helping to protect us against who-knows-what-that we could have picked in that bar bathroom.

Our day-long cultural orientation was complete. We were now headed for Kaya, a small town in the northeast part of the country, for French and local language training. For the next two months we "lived" the anticipated Peace Corps experience: no running water or electricity, and we lived in "banco" houses, houses built of mud bricks with a tin roof. Lighting at night was by kerosene lanterns. The water that we drank at mealtime was in recycled wine bottles and was treated with iodine tablets to kill the bacteria. It was always warm but saved us from dehydration, which at times seemed like a better alternative. We had yogurt, bread and either Nescafe or tea for breakfast every day we were there.

Showers were bucket showers in a banco hut that served as a shower room for both men and women, but at different times. Our toilets were creatively placed on a large field that separated our language classes from our living quarters. The toilet was a "hole" atop what can best be described as a giant ant hill or as a pitcher's mound, and it was surrounded by a wall of millet stalks. At least we didn't have to worry if the seat was left up or down,

We had started getting our first mandates (government checks) to be used at our discretion. Our discretion was to use the money to buy beer in the early evening after dinner at a local banco bar. We were desperate for anything resembling "cold." We had finally acclimated ourselves to the oppressive heat, but the thought of a cold drink was always on our minds. The bar served a beer called "Sovabra," and the beer came in large, dusty, green liter bottles. The beer was manufactured in Ouagadougou by a Russian company (we think), but it tasted like Heineken. It was great beer.

The bar across the dirt road from our training program had a unique way of cooling down the beers. They had giant clay canneries or giant clay pots. They were probably three feet high with a comparable diameter. The bar owners would fill the cannery with water, then place the beers down inside the giant container. Then they would wet the outside of the pot periodically throughout the day. The pots were placed under a tree, which also was somewhat of rarity. The air blowing against the wet cannery would gradually cool the water down inside the pot. By the end of the day, when we would wander in for a beer, I'm guessing that the temperature of the water had dropped to about 70 degrees. A 70-degree beer was a godsend and only got better with a second one.

Our language classes were held each morning in tents that were adjacent to one communal house that served as both a dining room and meeting area. On a scale of 0 to 10, with ten being able to speak fluently and effortlessly, my French was about .05 after eight weeks of training. Cass, on other the hand, had had four years of French in high school, and her ability to understand French speakers during our time in Africa was key to our very existence. How volunteers survived in many extreme living conditions over the course of their Peace Corps tour amazes me. I couldn't have done it by myself. We had one another to fall back on, but most of the volunteers flew solo.

The one other cultural enlightenment that both of us experienced during our eight-week training program was spending a weekend with a host family in Kaya. When I say "host family," it wasn't quite like living with a stereotypical middle-class family in America. These families were poor by anyone's standards, even in Upper Volta. It was an incredibly worthwhile experience, and I will always be appreciative of the families that we stayed with. I guess that 90% of the population of Upper Volta at that time had an average family income of $800 to $1,000 a year, and that's probably a stretch. The family that I stayed with was a traditional family. I stayed in a straw hut. The women would check in on me periodically and offer me water, and I remember eating a bowl of what can best be described as slimy, warm okra for dinner and maybe eating a (naturally) lukewarm porridge made of millet for breakfast. I can only assume that Peace Corps contracted with these families and paid them a small stipend to host us.

Everyone was nice regardless of language issues or cultural differences, and remember, I was white. I'm sure my host family had preconceived ideas about white people, but they were the majority race, and for the first time in my life I was minority. I really do not think race was a concern for these people. Their concern was survival, and whatever they got to provide us with this experience was much-needed household income. The highlight of the weekend for me was pounding millet with bare-breasted women, who just laughed at me doing my best to imitate their relentless motions of taking an elongated wooden pestle (approximately twenty lbs. in weight and six feet in length) and pounding it into a hand-made wooden mortar filled with millet, with the objective of turning this grain into flour. Unfortunately, I did not meet their high standards of throwing the heavy pestle up in the air, clapping, catching the pestle and pounding it into the mortar, but at least I provided a fun reprieve from the monotonous work of producing enough millet flour to feed their families.

Cass had a comparable experience with the host family with whom she stayed. We were both a source of curiosity for the people who lived in this rural community. People would come from all over just to look at us. Regardless, people were always nice, and if we helped them find a little joy in their lives at our expense, so be it. The first day Cass spent with her family she did her best to communicate with the women who were in her concession (living quarters). Although Upper Volta was a Christian country, there was still a significant number of Muslims living there, and having three or four wives was not uncommon; hence there always were a lot of women inhabiting a concession, none of whom spoke French. Cass spent much of her time communicating in gestures until the afternoon when one of the young daughters came home from school and could translate Cass's questions and needs into French.

Towards the end of our eight-week training in Kaya, we got word from the Peace Corps that there was a serious war going on in Chad, our intended destination. We were going to be in a program where we would help Chadians set up small businesses and teach them the different aspects of running them successfully. Aside from the sad fact that I'm sure many innocent people lost their lives or were seriously wounded as a result of that war, it turned out to be a great blessing for us. At first there was some concern that we would have to return home, and I can't say that this was devastating news for us at the time. Eight weeks of deprivation had taken its psychological toll on us, but at the same time the experience was starting to grow on us, and we saw other volunteers excited to be getting their work assignments in different areas of Upper Volta. When the Peace Corps offered us the option of going to Niger to work in the country's Youth Development Program, we became re-energized about the opportunity and opted to move ahead with our adventure.

After the training, all of the volunteers returned to Ouagadougou for a couple of days of rest and recovery before heading out to the towns and villages that they were assigned to. When Cass and I reached the Peace Corps hostel, we noticed a vintage Coke machine at the hostel headquarters. Using the Central African Franc coins (C.F.A.) that we had accumulated during our training program, we dropped the appropriate coins into the machine and, kerplunk, out came a typical green glass bottle of Coca-Cola, the same Coke that we knew from our childhood. It was ice cold! I cracked that top open and took a swig. It was the very best Coca-Cola that I have ever tasted in my life. Cass had a similar reaction. I remember my father telling me that at some point during World War II he was in Paris. For months he had eaten nothing but K-rations and whatever could be scraped together from the towns in which his train traveled. He bought a French baguette (which is in itself the best food one can eat in the world). One of the Army staples at that time was Spam. He said he opened his can of Spam, cut it into slices and placed it gingerly on the French baguette and took a giant bite. He told me that it was the best sandwich he had ever eaten in his life. Deprivation does that to you, but nonetheless, even today, a real French baguette and ice-cold Coca-Cola might be the best food and drink combination ever to tingle my palate.

We remained in Ouagadougou for about two months or so before going to Niger. The primary reason for the delay is that we were awaiting the arrival of a new group of volunteers from the States. When they arrived, we would become part of that group before getting assignments. The time in Ouagadougou was kind of nice. Like many African countries, the capital cities offered amenities that we were accustomed to in America. One of those amenities was the American Embassy, which included a swimming pool with an adjoining bar and a restaurant that served hamburgers. I know that part of our "raison d'être" was to try to assimilate within the culture, and ultimately we did a much better job of that, but at that moment we did succumb to cold beers as well as outdoor restaurants like the "The Guitar Bar" that grilled chicken on sheets of metal fencing over a wood-burning fire that made us forget eight weeks of deprivation in Kaya. Sensitivity to our new culture would have to wait for a couple of months.

The most amazing of all of the restaurants in Ouagadougou (actually, the most fascinating restaurant in West Africa) was the "L'Eau Vive"

(Water of Life). In the heart of Ouagadougou, adjacent to the main outdoor market (grande marche), was, for the lack of a better description, a line of one-story weathered buildings that looked like a tract mall that has seen its better days. In the very middle of this "mall," fifty feet from the marketplace with its fly-covered meats, vegetables and fruits, was this nondescript store-front restaurant that was operated completely by nuns. The L'Eau Vive was on the Peace Corps check list as a place that needs to be seen to be believed. If my memory serves me right, the restaurant opens every day at 7:00 p.m. To open during the day would've been futile, when it was always 95 to 100 degrees with market traffic and business, along with the beggars looking to find enough hand-outs to exist for another day; there was little chance of drawing customers. The restaurant served a decidedly French cuisine, and it catered primarily to expatriates and tourists. My assumption is that the proceeds from the nuns' efforts went to support whatever Catholic school existed in Ouagadougou, or maybe it existed simply support the nuns who worked there at night and in the schools during the day.

At any rate, the doors open at 7:00 p.m., and as you walk in, you have no idea what to expect. Immediately, you're shocked at the interior, which is immaculately clean, and the décor is decidedly French, with old religious paintings on the wall and similar artifacts placed within easy eyesight. The restaurant itself is, to our surprise, outdoors. You are led into an open courtyard with a white stone base for a floor where there are beautifully appointed tables with real damask tablecloths, fine silver wear and crystal glasses. When sun goes down, you can look up and see an incredible starlit sky while enjoying your meal. You are greeted by a nun, seated by a nun and served by a nun. We weren't risk-takers when it comes to food (although we did eat a lot of goat meat and okra in our training program in Kaya). We ordered the steak and fries (steak frites in French) avec a bottle (or maybe two) of red wine, and I believe we had some sort of French pastry for dessert. Did we feel a little guilty sitting there eating this fine French cuisine when outside this enclave there were people earning $2.00 a day, existing on rice and some kind of not particularly well-prepared tomato sauce? Well, admittedly there was some guilt, but It was a guilty pleasure to say the least.

Several years ago, I googled L'Eau Vive to see if it still exists, and it does. I wrote a recommendation on their website (the nuns have entered the 21st century). The recommendation is at the top of their reviews. You can Google it if you don't believe me. If this autobiography does not go over well, I will still be considered an internationally acclaimed restaurant critic.

After reviewing my account of our introduction to Africa, I realized that I failed to acknowledge our language teachers in Upper Volta. All them were hired by the Peace Corps to teach us both the French language as well as a local language or two. Cass did very well with her classes and I failed miserably but the language teachers were just the nicest people. I had the utmost respect for their conscientious efforts on our behalf. They were to be admired for their professionalism and they helped greatly in helping us to transition into a new and unfamiliar culture. They were the people that made us want to continue our journey. I wish I had stayed in contact with them over the years.

## Art Is in the Eye of the Beholder, or Don't Kick the Bucket

The Peace Corps set us up with a local batik artist who taught us how to make batiks with the idea of transferring those newly-learned skills to our Youth Development program in Niger. This was easy for Cass; after all, she did have an undergraduate degree in art from Towson University. For me, well, I sort of went along for the ride. My previous skills did not transfer so easily, but I did learn the process. One thing that I remember well from our batik training was how the wax was removed from the batik cloth. Hot wax is painted over the design and colors you have chosen, then the batik is dipped in boiling kerosene to remove the wax while leaving the design and colors on the material. That's the best explanation of the process I can offer, but the kerosene was what amazed me about the process. Our instructor would boil kerosene in a metal bucket over hot, burning coals. He put the fear of death in his kids not to get within fifty feet of the boiling bucket full of kerosene. Kerosene is harder to ignite than gasoline, but an errant spark had the potential for a massive explosion, and that was not lost on us as students. Cold beers and hamburgers at the American Embassy would have been more than an afterthought; it would've been an afterlife.

I took a lot of pictures when we went to Africa, but I didn't take a lot of notes. I'm fairly certain that we arrived in Niamey, Niger, from Ouagadougou in June of 1979. Initially we were housed with a group of Peace Corps volunteers who were there to be surveyors. Like a lot of Peace Corps volunteers at that time, these surveyors were learning surveying on the job in the Peace Corps. All of the Americans that we met in those years were adventurous and had joined the Peace Corps to try to make a difference in the lives of people in third world countries like Niger. In reality, in my opinion, the volunteers who made the most long-term difference were English teachers. Having the ability to speak a little bit of English would benefit the young who were fortunate to get a complete public education. The ability to speak English enabled them to have a chance to go to college in an English-speaking country as young adults, or to have a skill that might be useful in their own country working for the Nigerien government as it established economic relations with Anglophone countries like the United States.

Many of the other skills that volunteers had learned in the country simply turned into feel-good jobs at best. That sounds terrible, and I am generalizing a bit, but I do remember one volunteer in the fisheries program who was stationed in Diffa, the easternmost city in Niger on the Chadian border. His job was to tabulate the amounts and kinds of fish that were being taken by Nigerien fisherman on Lake Chad. There was one small problem. There was no water in Lake Chad in the area where he was assigned. The water had retreated to areas of the lake miles and miles from where he was posted. He was there for almost six months before anyone from Peace Corps checked on him, and I guess he was then reassigned to another similar program somewhere else in Niger that at least had a body of water that would support fish. My friend Keith Collier, a disgruntled volunteer who spent the first year of his time in Niger waiting for work in some kind of rural development program that never quite materialized, re-coined the Peace Corps motto of "The best job you'll ever love" to "The best job you'll never have." Keith transferred into the TEFL program (Teaching English as a Foreign Language) the second year he was there, and although he wasn't overly excited about teaching English, in the end he was among the volunteers who made a difference in the students' lives.

At the end of the day, Peace Corps is all about "public relations." Now, I know there are many current and former Peace Corps volunteers who would take great offense at such a statement, and of course that is their prerogative, but it is not my intention to disrespect the work they did or the experiences they had. I'm simply saying that the indigenous people in the countries that are served by the Peace Corps actually get to meet Americans, share their experiences and understand that the volunteers are good people just like them and remember them that way. They're not there to steal their country's resources or to patronize them. They are there to help out in any way they can. That is what makes Peace Corps a valuable asset.

Niamey as well as all of Niger was Muslim, and the differences between Ouagadougou and Niamey were noticeable as soon as we got off the plane. It also seemed as if Niamey was like a city caught in some sort of time warp. There were wide paved but sand-swept roads throughout the city. On one side of the road there were people driving cars, cabs, bikes and motorcycles, and on the other side there were Tuaregs riding camels that they had ridden that day from some remote town in the desert. Niger is a huge country geographically. The landscape of the entire country can only be described as a lunar landscape with the Sahara Desert covering most of the country. Niamey was also a cleaner city. It is located on the Niger River, which can be crossed on the water in a boat or on the Pont Kennedy (John F. Kennedy Bridge), which was a donation from the U.S. and completed in 1970. Nigeriens are extremely proud of this bridge and the positive connection between Americans and Nigeriens was evident during our years in Niger.

There was also the ubiquitous smell of the open concrete sewers that permeated your very being if you allowed it to do so, but after a time it became part of your sensory experience that was kind of irrelevant. People suffered the same level of poverty as Upper Volta, but because it was a Muslim country, people looked out for one another a little more. We noticed that people with disabilities were better cared for. There was still the pervasive chant of just about every person sitting on the side of whatever road you were on: "Anasara! Donne-moi un cadeau," which translates in the Hausa language to "White person, give me a gift (of money)," and many times we did. One of many things that I grew to understand while living in Niger was how lucky I was to have had the life that I had in America. While the chants were pervasive wherever we went, they were warranted. So many people had so little in their lives. I'm sure if I were in their place (I was going to write "shoes," but most had no shoes), I would have done the same.

Throughout my life I have always been in awe of "survivors," people who somehow make it through each day despite the hand they were dealt. Nigeriens as well as others from all parts of Africa and other third world countries have so many unfulfilled basic needs. It seems that with a little concerted effort, first world countries could collaboratively do enough to give these impoverished people a chance to lead a decent life. Wealthy countries in the world have the ability to do this, which would do little to affect their own standard of living other than to make them feel a little better about themselves.

We stayed in Niamey for another couple of months with our newly-arrived Youth Development Volunteers. After completing yet another language stage in both French and Hausa, we received our assignment. We were sent to Maradi, Niger, a small city of about 150,000 people on the northern-most border of Nigeria. I was assigned to a "C.E.G." (College d'Enseignement General) as a physical education teacher and basketball coach. A C.E.G. would be comparable to a middle school in the United States. The ages of the students (and the school was co-ed) were thirteen to sixteen years. Cass was assigned to a Maison Des Juenes, or Youth Center. She taught craft skills to young women who had come to the "big city" for a career. The goods these women made could then be sold in the marketplace. The underlying reason for Cass's program was to help deter these young ladies from becoming prostitutes. In 1980 a Muslim country like Niger did not offer too many options for women other than becoming the third or fourth wife of Nigerien men. Cass and I were regarded as nice people (Cass being much nicer than me) who were trying to make a difference.

Because of my limited French language skills, a lot of my teaching was done by offering examples of how to do something. My gestures worked relatively well and provided my students with a great deal of laughter. I taught basketball skills in the evening at an outdoor macadam court with sturdy metal basketball standards at both ends, standards that were built to withstand time as well as the weight of many people climbing on top of them to get a better view of the game. I coached both men and women, but later Cass added teaching the women players as well. She wasn't much of an offensive player, but I can attest first-hand that she had a tenaciousness about her when it came to defense.

The kids were really great. They were always testing their English language skills on me and would stop by our home in the evening to improve their speaking. I in turn would use my limited French on them. Their English was much better than my French.

Our house in Maradi was a single-story, four-room concrete block dwelling. We had electricity some of the time and running water some of the time. We even had indoor plumbing, including a shower. We had ceiling fans that when working would move the hot air around and humor the mosquitoes, whose reason to exist was to buzz around your ears and drive you nuts. We had no hot water, but it was 100 degrees almost every day. We had a kitchen with a gas stove that we'd fire up with a canister of gas that I would purchase every couple of months. I would carry this canister between my legs on my Peace Corps moped. People on the side of the road would watch with great anticipation of my crashing and exploding. Fortunately, their wishes never materialized.

We were living large not only by Nigerien standards but also by Peace Corps standards. A fair number of our friends lived in remote towns and villages with almost no amenities. Interesting too was that there were two other married couples in Maradi with similar living situations to us. We were envied by many, especially after they were living in the country for five or six months with little to eat other than rice and sauce or "mac and mac." Mac and mac was macaroni and mackerel sardines from a can. There was little to drink in the bush other than warm water, hot tea or Nescafe, if they were fortunate enough to have stocked up on these essentials when they passed through a small town on the way to their village.

We learned to be good hosts. There was one national highway that went from Niamey in the west through Maradi and on to Zinder, a comparable-size city in the eastern part of the country. The national highway was a two-lane road. The distance from Niamey to Zinder was about 465 miles, and we were at about the halfway mark. Most volunteers traveled on this highway in either bush taxies or on the SNTN national bus service. We became a weekend destination for many Americans. Maradi had bars and restaurants, and we were also within a short walking distance of *La Gare* (bus station). As a married couple we had the advantage of getting two checks a month, so we were able to purchase food and drinks that were either too expensive for the average volunteer or simply not available where they lived. We could buy fresh baked bread in the evenings, and there was a Lebanese grocery store where we could purchase canned meats or sardines, jams, those sorts of things. I always found it curious that throughout Africa there were Lebanese families who took root in all of these small cities and they were very successful, assimilating well with the local populations. The other item (and the most important) was that they sold wine.

For our parties we would buy a giant bidon of red wine that we'd serve in plastic coffee mugs (a ubiquitous item from China) to our weekend guests. When I say giant bidon, I'm talking a bottle that had the equivalent of five or six gallons of red wine. The cork on the bottle was about three inches in diameter. I would transport this bottle home on my moped as I did with the gas canister, placing the bottle between my legs and praying to Allah that it would not slip out as I rode about one mile to our home. Even Nigeriens were astounded at the dexterity I was able to display juggling this giant bottle seemingly effortlessly from the store to my maison. They were, however, somewhat disappointed that it wasn't gas canister day.

Now, this was not fine French wine by any standards known to man, much less, wine connoisseurs. It bordered on red wine vinegar but had an outstanding alcohol content. The first plastic coffee cupful was a bit hard to swallow, but if you could swallow a second cup, it started tasting much better, and if you were still standing for the third go-around, you would've arrived at fine red wine.

In some way, shape or form we probably hosted these "soirees" (parties) about once a month. Communication was by word of mouth. If I wanted to let people know in advance, I would write some notes, put them in separate envelopes and go to the bus station to find "carrier pigeons." These were Nigerien young people who would be traveling to or through a particular town along the way. I would give them a note and probably what amounted to $1.00 and ask them if they could find a particular volunteer in the town where they were going and deliver the note. There was a degree of trust involved in this process to be sure, but invariably the messages always got to the intended recipients. Volunteers who received the messages would get a bush taxi on the following weekend and head to Maradi for (less than) vintage wine and a short reprieve from deprivation. We have stayed in touch with many of these former volunteers over the last forty-some years, and we host a party every decade where thirty to forty volunteers plus their extended families come to Mt. Airy, Maryland, from literally all parts of the world.

We had a lot of success stories during the two years we lived in Maradi. We met a lot of really nice Nigeriens in addition to the American volunteers who came to our city. It is interesting that Niger is 99% Muslim (and coincidentally we lived right next door to a Baptist Church). There never were any problems whatsoever related to racial or religious differences. Cass could travel in a bush taxi by herself throughout the country and never feel a sense of fear. I think the biggest takeaway here is that people are the same regardless of their origin or their beliefs or even their economic situations. Everyone has hopes and dreams of a better life.

During the second year we were there, my boys' basketball team started exhibiting some skills. I attribute a lot of their success to my predecessor George Russell, a volunteer who came before Cass and I got there. George was well-schooled, was knowledgeable about basketball, and I think he got the players to the point where they were starting to play well. He was very passionate about being a Peace Corps Volunteer, and it was his mission to teach these kids to be fundamentally good players. I think what I did was just work with the players to improve on the skills that George had taught them, and that enabled them to be even better players. We went to the national high school sports festival at the end of my second year. It was called the Championnat Scolaire and was held in Diffa at the far edge of the eastern part of Niger. All of the towns which had C.E.G.s participated. It was a four-day event, necessitated by the traveling in bush taxis from all parts of Niger.

As I recall, the Championnat Scolaire also included a national "Lute" match. Lute is a traditional form of wrestling in Niger, kind of like Sumo wrestling but without fat people. The participants are men in their 20's and 30's who had grown up doing manual labor on farms. Every one of them seemed to be six feet tall and about 245 lbs. There was not an ounce of fat on any of these men. Superman (or Chief Strongbow) would have had his hands full with any one of these guys. The match is conducted on a marked circular area about thirty feet in diameter. As I recall, the objective is to lock arms and try to throw your opponent out of the circle from a standing position. For all the ferociousness that the lutteurs emit as they attack one another, it's a pretty civil form of combat. Each luter is rewarded with handfuls of money given by rich "fonctionaires" (businessmen) if they win a match from a particular fonctionaire's region. Here's the reason for including this. I traveled to the tournament in a van that as I recall may have even had air conditioning. Cass, who was helping to coach the girls' basketball team in addition to being responsible for setting up her female entrepreneurs' knitting projects, traveled with the lutteurs in this rundown bus with no windows. She rode in the back seat. When we arrived at the site, Cass exited the van covered with red dust from the Sahara Desert and surrounding lunar landscape. Her glasses were opaque. We slept that night on the lunar landscape with nothing but the stars above us, but she wasn't as awed by the starlit sky as she otherwise may have been. I guess she forgot to clean her glasses.

Our basketball team won the national tournament, a big deal for the players. Under normal circumstances my players played basketball either in their bare feet or in flip-flops. Several months before the season-ending tournament, I mentioned the lack of basketball shoes in a letter that Cass sent to her sister Julie (the Hutzler's photographer) and her husband Bruce, who was a Presbyterian minister in Parkersburg, West Virginia. Bruce told my story and solicited the community for money to buy basketball shoes. About a month before the tournament, a representative from the American Embassy in Niamey showed up at our house in Maradi with a huge cardboard box of Converse All-Star sneakers in varying sizes and more than enough for my players. When I got them together, they were absolutely ecstatic! At that point we still had about three weeks before the tournament. For the entire three weeks of practice leading up to the Championnat, the players still practiced in their bare feet or flip-flops. They didn't want to dirty their shoes before the games.

Bruce, Julie and their daughter Sarah actually visited us in Maradi during our two-year stint there. They became part of our African experience. During our time there another friend, Karen Petronio, and her friend visited us. We've always been appreciative of all of them taking that time from their lives to visit us and understand our experiences.

I have to fast forward here again to 2021. On May 23, 2021, my brother-in-law, Bruce Baker died after suffering through a terrible neurological illness. I have the most utmost respect for people who treat others regardless of their differences as they would like to be treated. Bruce was one of those people. He practiced what he preached. He will be greatly missed but remembered fondly by all who knew him. The players I coached did not know him but he played an integral part in their winning a championship.

I have a couple more stories to squeeze in here. They might upset the flow of the storyline, but if you've suffered through my story to this point so I think you realize that the ebb and flow of this book would test the seaworthiness of my father's 18' canoe.

Special occasions during our time in Niger were acknowledged, but on a different scale. For one of my birthdays Cass went to a tailor in town to buy me a "grand boo boo," a flowing kind of African shirt that was both colorful and comfortable. The tailor could only speak Hausa. Cass, always the experienced linguist, explained to him that I was very tall and the shirt would have to have very long sleeves. "Tall" in Hausa is "Dogo." I also had a long beard at that time. "Beard" in Hausa is "Gemi." The term for me was "Dogo Mai Gemi," or tall man with beard. Cass explained that I had long arms. That was what the tailor had to work with. She went back a couple of days later to pick up the finished product. It was a beautiful, well-tailored shirt. There was, however, a distinguishing feature. The arms of the shirt were literally about forty-eight inches in length. Cass, while astonished, did not want to embarrass the tailor. She paid for the shirt and complimented him on his work. She brought the shirt home and I tried it on. I looked like one of those inflatable noodles that you see in current times in front of a gas station or used-car lot to drum up business. I wish I had kept that shirt for posterity's sake, but I believe I left it behind for another tall Nigerien with a beard and extremely long arms.

On the flip side of gift-giving, on the first Christmas that we spent in Niger we took a bush taxi trip to an ancient city called Agadez in the northern part of Niger in the Sahara Desert. Agadez was founded in the 14th century and was a major trade route for medieval caravans crossing the Sahara. There are still caravans of camels that bring salt from an area called Bilma. When we visited Agadez at night during Christmas of 1980, it could've been Bethlehem. It was a small city of buildings all made out of mud. The streets between the buildings were sand pathways. The air was warm but slightly on the cool side. There was no breeze. The sky was absolutely crystal clear. I can't imagine a place on earth where the stars are just as brilliant as they were in

Agadez. All of the homes were lit by kerosene lanterns, and the smell was subtle enough that it provided a pleasing odor that complemented the ancient surroundings.

Peace Corps volunteers who lived in town arranged for us to stay in one of the mud homes provided for them. We had been traveling the entire day to get there from Niamey and were exhausted. It was a cool evening by Agadez standards. I had not gotten Cass a Christmas gift. There was a building where we could take a bucket shower. I bartered with a local resident to put a bucket of water on an outdoor fire that they had built for warmth. When the water was significantly warm, I took it to where Cass and I were staying, presented the bucket of hot water to her and said, "Merry Christmas." It was the first hot shower she had had in quite some time. It didn't seem like much of a gift then, but Cass has remembered this all these years later, so I guess I must have made a favorable impression on her that evening.

Agadez was also known for its jewelry-making. I also bought Cass a Cross of Agadez, which was probably made out of a Land Rover bumper found on the side of the road from a crash that probably had occurred weeks before. Despite the origin of the metal used in the jewelry, it was well-crafted and very pretty and she still has this keepsake. The cross was a symbol of the Mosque of Agadez, which was made of mud and has been standing in the center of the city since it was built in the 15th century.

When we were ready to leave Agadez that weekend, we made a connection somehow with a trucker who was headed to Zinder, another interesting city about 250 miles to the west of Maradi in Eastern Niger. I can't remember the particulars, but one of the other volunteers who was headed in the same direction asked the trucker for a ride and told him we would be willing to pay for a lift. Money sometimes talks and it spoke to this driver. Now, this was a tractor trailer kind of truck with a bed full of grain in the back. We were told we could climb up and ride in the grain. Here we were, riding through the desert in the back of a six-wheeler, eight or ten American Peace Corps volunteers on top of tons of grain. It was the best ride that we had during our two-and-a-half years in Niger. Could this tractor and trailer have turned over on what can best be described as just barely a two-lane macadam road with barely enough macadam to support such a vehicle? Yes, but we burrowed into the grain, silently praying to Allah that we would survive the journey. We did.

The stories of our time and experiences in Niger could go on and on, and I would love to be able to tell them, and maybe I will in the sequel to "Obits and Pieces." Our time in Africa was coming to an end after twenty-nine months. I do have one last entry that no doubt will enlighten you ("enlighten," of course, being yet another one of those relative terms). Niger's lifeblood revolved around the outdoor marketplaces throughout the country. The common thread of all the markets was that you had to bargain for every single item you wanted to purchase; no price tags in La Grande Marche. It was simply a part of the culture, and everybody was subjected to the process and understood it, except for foreigners. To us it was an insane but necessary endeavor if one wished to purchase anything. Let's say, for example, that you wanted to buy a mango. First of all, mangoes in Niger were as plentiful if not more plentiful than the apples produced on that one apple tree in the backyard of my youth. Mangoes were everywhere, and women with baskets full of them would sit side-by-side in the market trying to sell them. There were different types of mangoes, but in the big scheme of things a mango was a mango.

The process began this way. You first had to greet the seller every time. Even if you had to greet the seller next to your first vendor, it all had to start over again. In Hausa, "Ina Kwana?" ("How did you sleep?") The vendor on cue would respond, "La Hiya Lo." ("Fine, I slept in health.") Then you would ask, "Ina ga giya?" ("How is your tiredness?") The vendor would respond, "Ba gagiya." ("There is no tiredness.") I've always suspected this to be a lie. Sitting there all afternoon under a tree would certainly have been cause for a nap. By the same token, the vendor did say she slept in health. This exchange would go on, and then you'd ask the vendor, "How much for this mango?" and the vendor would respond in Hausa language, "$5.00." Now, the mango was worth a nickel, so you began this back-and-forth jabber for what seemed like forever until both sides finally relented and you got the mango for two nickels. The vendor was happy because she got double what she expected, and the buyer was exhausted that he had to go through all of this for a mango. Such is life in the Sahel.

One of the purchases that could be made at the markets was clothing that had been shipped to the country from churches and other non-profits in the United States that collected donations in their communities for the specific purpose of providing clothing in poor countries. These clothes were sent to shipping companies to be distributed to various port locations throughout Africa. Entrepreneurs on the destination end would purchase lots of these clothes, separate them and sell them for nominal fees in these marketplaces. They are sold for very little to people who have very little to spend but who would cherish these purchases. One day in Maradi we saw a young boy with a t-shirt that actually read "Give me the City Life," and it had a picture of Baltimore row houses on the front of the shirt. It made us a bit homesick. We were ready to head home.

The poem below is a tribute to the young basketball players with whom I worked in Niger. Looking back on those times, they now seem very exotic and they were. The Nigerien people whom we met as well as the Peace Corps Volunteers with whom we worked and the experiences that we had were like no other.

## Reflection: Earwigs and Basketball

I will not miss the earwigs;
The sand, the dust, the heat.
They landed on my shoulders
And crawled down to my feet.

And when I tried to teach my players
The game of basketball,
They'd settled gently on my ears,
Around which they would crawl.
Maybe they were shouting,
As I tried so hard to teach
A proper pass, a pick and roll,
"In French please," they would screech.

I tried again, in French this time,
They did not heed my call.
They picked, they rolled, their flip-flops flopped,
Each time they lost the ball.

As time went on, they got much better;
Their skills they did improve.
They practiced every day and night.
They finally found their groove.

The earwigs seemed not to notice
The improvement in the team.
As I look back and remember them,
They're still a nightmarish dream.

My memories of my players though,
Will remain always very good.
They worked hard and won a championship;
The earwigs and I knew they would.

## Out of Africa

We packed up our clothes, souvenirs and other belongings in our duffle bags, and we prepared to leave our home of two years in Maradi, Niger. It's funny how our perspective on things had changed in that time. We actually were considering staying for another year. We had been away from home for almost 2 ½ years. In those days, communication home was done by "snail mail." There were no cell phones or computers. Our communication to our parents and friends was usually a two-to three-week turn-around, and when we received letters or packages, well, those were special days. We once received a post card from a friend of ours in Baltimore City that astounded us. The card was from Lynn Daughtry. Lynn was a young Black disabled man from a really poor area of East Baltimore. Lynn had cerebral palsy. His mobility was limited but he could use both a wheelchair as well as walk independently for short distances if he had to.

For someone who was so disabled he had an exorbitant amount of self-confidence. His ability to speak and be understood was a challenge to all that knew him but his persistence in being understood was never lost on anybody and ultimately, we would get the drift. Lynn considered me to be his Godfather. We received this postcard from Lynn that had a postmark of two weeks prior to us receiving the card. The writing on the card was barely legible and how he got our address is still a mystery. It had an eleven-cent regular postage stamp; not an airmail stamp. The only explanation for us getting that post card was that his persistence somehow became telepathic and it was somehow transferred to the U.S. Postal Service.

Lynn is another one of those people who has passed on since those times in Niger but he too was a survivor. He could have come to West Africa for a visit, ingratiated himself to whomever he met, and he would have survived as if he had lived in West Africa all of his life.

During our second year we received a letter from my mother which said that Jack seemed to be doing okay after his heart attack. Whoa! What's happening here? I was in shock. We needed to be able to call home. I have no idea what time it was on the east coast of the United States when we made the call, but we went to the post office that afternoon in Maradi and inquired if we could make a long-distance call to my home in America. When I was finally able to explain my dilemma in French to the ladies who worked at the post office (Cass was again the savior here), after a two-hour wait, miraculously I heard my home phone ring and heard Hazel's voice on the other end. She was as astounded as I was. I explained about the letter we received and asked her about Jack's condition. He was doing fine. A month had passed since the attack occurred. It was so great to hear Hazel's voice. I don't want to say I was emotional, so I won't say it, but I was a basket case. I told Hazel we'd be home soon, and the call ended. I thanked the ladies at the post office profusely. What they did for me that day words could not express; and if they could, I don't think these ladies would have understood anyway and my French would have only made them laugh.

After that call we no longer had reservations about leaving. We were ready to go. We said our good-byes to the Nigerien family that took up residence in our yard when we first arrived two years before. They were our unofficial guardians. In return for our letting them build a straw house in our yard and use our outdoor water faucet, they guarded our house against intruders. The life that these people lived was incredibly simple.

I was reminded while writing this about the head of this household (or straw-hut hold). The man was known as a "mai shai," a seller of tea. His earnings from selling hot tea infused with lait-sucre (sweetened canned milk) at the bus stop each morning somehow kept the family functioning with the basic necessities of life. I remember one day when there was some national event in Maradi. I knew the bus lot would be full of travelers from all over Niger. I was happy for the "mai shai" because I figured it would afford him an opportunity to make a lot of money for his family; however, he came back into our concession at the same time he did every morning, around 10:30 a.m. I asked him why he came home so early. Wasn't this a chance for him to make a lot of money? He replied that he had made the amount of money he needed that day to feed his family. That was all he needed. What about tomorrow, I asked? "Allah will provide," he said. Living in the moment was all that was important.

On the morning we left our home, we gave the family some gifts, wished them well and went off to the bus yard to get a bush taxi to Niamey, an eight- to ten-hour trip. I do wonder what became of this family. Their children were all under five years old when we were there. They would now be in their mid-forties. I hope that by their standards they had a good life.

## The Journey Home

When we arrived in Niamey, we made our flight arrangements. Our plan was to spend a month traveling in Europe before heading back to the States. The Peace Corps set aside "readjustment" money for volunteers who had completed their service. It was more than enough at the time to travel a bit before heading home and was a much-appreciated perk. I remember in the first months after we arrived in Niger seeing people who had completed their Peace Corps service and were heading home, and we were so envious. Now it was our turn.

After spending a few days in Niamey to get our affairs in order, we said our goodbyes to the volunteers that we had known in Niamey and boarded an Air Afrique DC-10 to Marseilles, France. We had a short stopover in Algiers before heading across the Mediterranean to the second-largest city in France.

When asked by other volunteers about travel plans, we'd say we were going to take the "industrial tour" through Europe. Coming from a blue-collar industrial city like Baltimore, we explained, it was a way to help us transition back into our previous life. In reality we took an amazing "tourist tour" through the south of France, Italy, up through the French Alps to Germany, on to the Netherlands and then back down to Paris for our return to the United States.

## Two Days of Bouillabaisse

When we disembarked from our plane in Marseilles, we were immediately struck by the reality of coming back into the modern world. Niger had some modern amenities, but for the most part there were areas that had not significantly changed in centuries. There were still Tuareg caravans that functioned as they had functioned 300 years earlier.

Marseilles had an almost "Disneyland" effect on our psyche. It was obviously a very old European city, but there were paved streets, bustling crowds and no outward signs of abject poverty. There were real bars and restaurants packed with families enjoying themselves without the concern of how they would pay for their meals. There were churches and modern buildings, and there were also beautiful old European apartment buildings with running water and real toilets. We did a two-day "bouillabaisse" tour of the city. Bouillabaisse is of course the seafood dish for which Marseilles is best known. We ordered this for our first dinner at a local restaurant located within eyesight of the Mediterranean to add to the authenticity of the moment. The bouillabaisse was very good. It was not something that blew me away after two-and-a-half years of rice and sauce, but Cass and I both enjoyed the food and the experience.

Before we left, we ran into Roger Shands and Mark "Sully" Sullivan in the hotel where we were staying. They were part of our Youth

Development group in Niger and were also heading home. It just seemed like such a coincidence running into them in a foreign country. It was a quick reminder that they too had just left this same world from which we had come, and they too were now a part of this readjustment period that we were also experiencing. Needless to say, they were surprised to see us as well.

## Nice Is Nice (Really Nice)

We stayed in Marseilles for two or three days before boarding a train for Nice, France. We had a friend there, Louis Cagnol, whom we had met in Niger while he was visiting a Peace Corps friend of ours, Mike Klinger. Louis had a great time with our friend Klinger and had the added advantage of being French. He made friends easily with Nigerien and other French-speaking teachers from Francophone countries in West Africa who were teaching in the many small towns throughout Niger.

Mike Klinger taught English in small town called Guidan Roumdji. He too could speak fluent French and Spanish with a little Arabic thrown in for good measure. He had a great sense of humor, and his interactions with his African colleagues always had them laughing. I always envied his linguistic abilities. Mike is an example of why I said Peace Corps is more a public relations exercise than anything else. Klinger was also an English teacher, so he really made an impact.

Nice was really "nice." I have photographs from my father which indicate that he had been there during WWII. There was this weird nostalgic kind of feeling being in Nice. We made our way to a hotel where Louis met us. It was so good to see him. Now, Louis was not multi-lingual like our mutual friend Klinger. He could speak French and we could speak English. Cass was the intermediary, and although she struggled a bit in French, it was passable enough that we could enjoy one another's company. Nice was more than "nice." It was beautiful!

Louis gave us an incredible walking tour of the tourist areas, including towns that were over a thousand years old.

Louis really showed us a "nice" time. He took us to a blues and jazz festival that included Muddy Waters, Chick Correa and Miles Davis among other world-class musicians. It was incredible! Music was another deprivation area in Niger. The music we got on the BBC or Voice of America on our short-wave radio left a lot to be desired, and I don't want to be culturally insensitive, but traditional Nigerien music was extremely hard on the auditory senses.

We still keep in touch with Louis. I have a Peace Corps distribution list that I use to contact our Peace Corps friends and Louis as well as our German friends Helga and Johannes Marx, who were in Niger in the German equivalent of the Peace Corps and who we would visit later on our European excursion.

## Rub the Pig's Nose (and You'll Have Great Luck)

After spending three or four days in Nice, we thanked our host Louis and headed for our next destination, which was Florence, Italy. Florence is a beautiful city; I guess that's one of those understatements. I am not a museum goer, but Cass had an art background and was not going to pass up an opportunity to see some of the finest historic art in the world, including the statue of David at the Accademia Gallery, Botticelli's *The Birth of Venus* and paintings by Da Vinci, Rembrandt and Michelangelo at the Uffizi Gallery. While I may have gotten a "B" in Art Appreciation (possibly a B-), I lacked the art "appreciation" factor. Nonetheless I went with Cass to all of the museums and did a good job of acting like I was really interested, and I was, but the thrill was not quite the same as Cass's. My biggest thrill was being able to rub the nose of the *Porcellino*, the bronze pig in the center of the city which was sculpted by Pietro Tacca shortly before 1634 (I knew this from

Art Appreciation 101) that tourists rub for good luck. Now THAT was a beautiful piece of art.

There were a couple more interesting things about Florence that warrant a brief comment. The bridges for which the city is known were the architectural wonders that included the Ponte Vecchio, the Ponte alla Carraia and the Ponte alle Grazie among others. A final note of interest is that wine was cheaper to buy than bottled water.

## Biergarten

Having done Florence, Cass and I mounted another train that included a couple of transfers along the way, with our next destination being Munich. Trains are great transportation. It's a shame that we do not have a comparable system in the U.S., but I digress. We passed through the French Alps along the way. They appeared as they appear in photographs—tall, snow-covered and breath-takingly beautiful.

We were about two-and-a-half weeks into our whirlwind industrial tour when we arrived in Munich, Germany, West Germany at that time, in July of 1981. Including several countries in Africa, we were seeing areas of the world that we most likely would never have seen if not for our decision to join the Peace Corps. I do not recall a whole lot about Munich except for the beer gardens, and they very well may be the reason I remember little. Munich was as advertised, and the lederhosen-clad people lived up to the billing. We consumed a significant amount of beer out of very large steins. We assumed that we were expected to drink large quantities of beer, and we certainly did not want to offend our German hosts. Munich had checked all of the boxes.

On a much more serious note, we took the time to visit the Dachau Concentration Camp while we were there. That was a very humbling and incredibly sad experience. We also visited Anne Frank's House in

Amsterdam after we left Germany. It is difficult to describe the emotions that take hold of you when confronted with the realities of what occurred in these places.

We took another train from Munich to Cologne, Germany, to visit our friends Helga and Johannes Marx. Besides German, they both could speak French and English, which always amazed me as I struggled to get my French to 1.5 on the 1 to 5 scale. (When I think about it, my English is probably only a 2 out of 5.) At any rate, we befriended one another along the way, and that friendship extends to today.

When we arrived in Cologne, the first thing I noticed was the "Eau de Cologne" sign on the train station entrance. Honestly, I thought Eau de Cologne was a topical perfume that my parents and grandparents used. I didn't think the product still existed.

Helga and Johannes were wonderful hosts. They gave us a walking tour of the city. In terms of its buildings and infrastructure, Cologne was new. It had been bombed to dust during World War II. Other than a few churches that were spared by the grace of God (who saved the churches but couldn't strike Hitler with a bolt of electricity), all the buildings were rebuilt after the war. Johannes pointed out a gargoyle at the top of one these buildings that apparently had become a tourist attraction. "See that gargoyle up there, Mike? That's a 'shyster.' " A shyster, he informed me, meant "shitter" in English, and sure enough, that was how the shyster was sculpted at the top of the building.

They also took Cass and me to a German restaurant that sat above the Rhine River. The restaurant served Pilsner beer in fragile beautifully-designed thin fluted glasses. I guess these glasses would hold about 10 oz. of beer. Having overindulged in beer drunk from giant steins in Munich, I was obliged to restrain myself. Johannes knew what I was thinking; he knew Americans had a propensity to down large quantities of beer at one sitting that were disproportionate to what their bodies were designed to hold. The experience at the restaurant was an enjoyable time, and we were appreciative of Helga and Johannes being such welcoming hosts.

## The Heineken Experience

Next up: Amsterdam. We hopped on another train after saying our goodbyes to Helga and Johannes and headed for the city of elaborate canals, Heineken beer and store-front brothels. Like all European capitals, Amsterdam was a beautiful city, and, like other cities that we had visited, had a unique quality. It was the first city that we had been to since we left the States in 1979 where English was widely spoken. It was nice to order a meal in a bar or restaurant without having to struggle to say what we wanted.

Amsterdam was ahead of its time on the environment. Almost everyone rode a bike as a necessary form of transportation as opposed to a ride in the park. The ladies in the store-front brothels certainly stoked the imagination of more than a few male tourists as they politely waved to the maidens-in-waiting behind the glass windows.

We felt compelled to visit the house of Anne Frank. When we went into the house, we felt the spirits of those who had lived in that house and thought about how unfair and unjust it was that Anne had been the victim of such a horrible ending. At times like this, I cannot imagine what would have been going through the minds of my own grandchildren had they lived such a life: the fear of not knowing what would happen to them; the terrible loneliness of not having your family there to support you; and of course, the fear of death which was inevitable. To this day when I see a documentary listed on PBS about Anne Frank or see the book *The Diary of Anne Frank,* it causes a lump in my throat. I can't watch the documentary or even consider reading her diary again. Visiting that house was a stark reminder of man's inhumanity to man—and women and children.

Cass and I spent three or four days in Amsterdam. Before we left, I do vaguely remember going to the Van Gogh Museum and to the Rijksmuseum, which held paintings by Rembrandt and Vermeer among others. Again, I went to these museums with Cass, who was just ecstatic to see such original works of art. Cass asked me what I thought of one of Rembrandt's paintings, and I was complimentary. I said, "They're pretty good."

## City of Lights

We paid our respects to Amsterdam and headed for the train station for what we believed would be the next-to-last adventure before heading home, Paris, the City of Lights. We thought that London would have been our final departure point, but when we arrived in Paris, it was at the same time as Charles and Diana's wedding in Great Britain. There were few flights to London and no hotel rooms available there, so we decided that Paris would be our jumping-off point and that we'd stay a little longer as a result of having additional time and still enough money to go out with a bang. It was time and money well spent.

Paris remains our favorite city of all of those that we visited in Europe. Since that visit in 1981 we have been back three times, and we tentatively are planning to go back again for our 50th wedding anniversary in 2022, assuming that COVID-19 has run its course and the political climate in France has improved. Paris feels like one of those "time warp" cities, not like the time warp as I described it in Niger, but there is just something magically nostalgic about the place that gives you the impression you're experiencing layers of history wherever you go; and each layer takes you back to a time and place which, for some inexplicable reason, allows you to be part of that layer for the brief time you're there. The 2011 movie "Midnight in Paris" does a pretty good job of capturing this feeling.

The Luxembourg Gardens (Les Jardins du Luxembourg) were a perfect example of this. Here was a garden that was completed in 1625 but did not meet its current dimensions until 1790. Whew! Talk about time travel. When we arrived in Paris from Amsterdam, we stayed in a hotel that was close to Le Jardins du Luxembourg. The garden was a suggested tourist attraction and it was on our travel itinerary. When we first walked into Le Jardins, it was almost surreal. To me it was like an old French postcard. There was the toy boat lake with kids actually moving their boats with long sticks. There were people dressed for the occasion. It was the latter part of July 1981 and it was hot, but nothing like the heat in Niger, and there were beautiful trees for cover. There were men, mostly older men, playing boules, which is similar to bocce in Italy. There were mothers with baby carriages who seemed so at ease pushing the carriages and then sitting down on a park bench just to relax, talk with friends and enjoy their surroundings. There were little bistros throughout the park where you could buy sandwiches, coffee, wine and desserts. You'd sit at a table and a waiter would come by, take your order and make you feel kind of special.

I have mentioned this to people before, but it wasn't just that my French was intolerably bad; it was my accent. The waiter in the park, for example, had a puzzled look on his face when I spoke, not because of my bad French but because I had an African accent. All the French teachers I had in Niger were Africans. So here I am, a middle-aged white American sounding like a Black African who obviously hadn't worked hard on his French when growing up in sub-Saharan Africa. When all was said and done, though, we got our sandwiches and glasses of wine and life was good.

The absolute best sandwich in Paris is the famous croque monsieur, a delicious sandwich of toasted ham and cheese which despite its simplicity is somehow a culinary delight. When you have that with an ice-cold Coca Cola (never as cold or refreshing as that first coke in

Ouagadougou, mind you, but pretty close) while sitting under a tree with French music playing in the background, you lose your sense of living in the present. You imagine yourself sitting in the same place in the 1920's. I wouldn't necessarily want to be sitting around with Gertrude Stein or Ernest Hemingway, but just enjoying French accordion music with a glass of red wine and watching the people of that time drift up and down on the Avenue des Champs-Elysees, that would be pleasant.

After I spent two-and-a-half years in the desert, in my humble opinion the French baguette you could buy in France for $1.50 at your local boulangerie each morning and have with French roast coffee with cheese and fruit are the best examples of French cuisine available to mankind. You can keep your goose liver paté and escargot. I am quite content with the basics, merci beaucoup.

Paris is obviously a tourist haven. I have no problem with that; I'm a tourist. People get caught up in seeing things that the tourists don't see, or maybe they've been to Paris, maybe have even lived in Paris for time, and have this smugness that seeing Notre Dame or the Eiffel Tower or the Rodin Museum or Montmartre is somehow beneath them. We have been to Paris four times, and on each visit, I spend time at the aforementioned landmarks, and each time I find myself in awe of my surroundings. I love these places.

Notre Dame is certainly the "mother," in a manner of speaking, of all of Paris's churches. It is an architectural wonder, but my favorite is Sacre-Coeur Basilica, which sits at the top of Montmartre and looks out over the City of Paris. St. Michael the Archangel is prominently displayed inside the church, which adds to my bias, but there really is something that approaches "spiritual" when you sit on the front steps of that church.

Paris contains some of the finest museums in the world, and I believe Cass and I have been to most of them. The Louvre of course is the best known and surely the most visited. There were many occasions at the Louvre when Cass would point out a work of great art that she had seen only in art books. She would ask my opinion, and I would respond in a very serious and seemingly appreciative voice, "That's pretty good."

The subway system in Paris is the best public transportation system I've ever been on. You can never get lost in Paris if you understand the system. Within the framework of Paris proper, there is always a subway stop where you can mount a train that will, with a transfer here and there, get you back from whence you came.

Paris is another of those special places in our lives that I could write pages about. Unfortunately, time is of the essence (my copy editor is becoming impatient), and we need to catch our flight home. Paris, however, will again pop up unexpectedly in future chapters, so please don't feel short-changed.

## Home again, Home again, Jiggity-Jig

Our flight home from Paris was uneventful other than the excitement and anticipation of seeing our parents, family and friends again. It was now August of 1981. My brother- and sister-in-law Bob and Trish Hemler, the guardians of our house in our absence for two-and-a-half years, met us at the airport. With them were Cass' parents, Mare and Char. Cass' parents were absolutely thrilled to see us. I can't remember if we landed in Baltimore or D.C

Our readjustment allowance, the money that we had used to travel through Europe after leaving the Peace Corps, was to help volunteers when they returned to the States and needed to get reestablished with a job, a place to live or whatever would benefit them in returning to the world they once knew. Some volunteers, even Cass and I included to some extent, did have a difficult time adjusting when they returned home. While family and friends were glad to see them and would have questions about their experiences, their own lives had not changed and the world they were living in is what they were comfortable with. They simply could not relate to the experience, and after they asked their questions, life went on. We, on the other hand, had had experiences that changed our perspective on life. So initially returned volunteers were understandably concerned about their immediate futures. Once they got jobs or went back to college, things started to get back to the normal life they once knew. Many of these volunteers got jobs with foreign service branches of the government like U.S.A.I.D. (United States of America International Development), and some went back to school to get advanced degrees related to international development and upon graduating found employment in developing nations, providing more specific help with areas of dire need in those countries.

Cass and I were more fortunate. We not only had a home that we owned to come back to, but also jobs with organizations in which we previously worked. I went back to the League for People with Disabilities for about six months. Chad Casserly, a friend and co-worker from when I worked at the League in the previous decade, had become the Director of Camping and Recreation at the League after my departure and offered me an assistant's position to help me transition back into the mainstream. I only mention Chad because if he should read this book that I'm in the process of putting together, he'd be upset if his name didn't appear. Regardless, Chad has been a good friend over the years, and his offering me a job upon my return to the States was greatly appreciated.

## Next Step

Cass went back to the nursing facility where she previously worked (former home of the James Brown Motor Inn). One of her colleagues was Jo Cason. In later years, Jo Ann became a colleague of mine at the Baltimore City Department of Recreation and Parks. I was the Program Coordinator for the Therapeutic Recreation Division, and she was the Program Coordinator for the Seniors Division. We both knew Ralph Jones well, and both of us had the same Master's Degree in Urban Recreation from the University of Baltimore.

When Jo worked with Cass, they planned recreation programs for the residents of the nursing facility. The residents always fascinated me because they were also survivors. Most of them also had underlying mental illnesses. They all had ways to "get by." At that time smoking was not prohibited in facilities like this, and smoking, while being the least of these folks' problems, was a personal as well as recreational activity for the vast majority. Because no one had much money for cigarettes, they were a much-valued commodity. There was one industrious lady who would use her monthly stipend from the State of Maryland to buy cigarette wrappers. Throughout the day she would move around the facility and collect used cigarette butts, come back to her room, tap out the unsmoked tobacco, put it into a bowl and then use it to roll "generic" cigarettes that she would then resell to other residents. These folks epitomized the term "survivors."

It was just a cast of fascinating people. I remember Cass showing me a drawing done by a resident with severe schizophrenia. The drawing was of a lion. It was done I believe in pen and ink. It was Picasso-like. It truly was a brilliant piece of art and it been done by a brilliant person whose mind was constantly in distress. This was the life he was given and this was the life that through no fault of his own he had to live. If you are fortunate enough to live a long and prosperous life, appreciate the ability to see, to hear, to walk unencumbered, to think clearly and make the time to give back to people who are limited by the hand they were dealt, you have been blessed. Some folks aren't as lucky.

After a short time at the nursing facility, Cass found new employment as a Recreational Therapist with the Veteran's Administration at Fort Howard in Dundalk, Maryland and I saw an employment ad in *The Baltimore Sun* for a position as a Therapeutic Recreation Specialist at Lutheran Hospital in West Baltimore. The job was in an acute care psychiatric wing of the hospital. I had absolutely no experience whatsoever working with people who had to cope with mental illness, but that did not discourage me from applying for this job. I could do this. How hard could it be?

Let me say this, it was challenging. The unit where I worked provided services for both adults and adolescents. My biggest hurdle was understanding the adolescents. I had worked with disabled people who, despite their limitations, found ways to compensate and have successful lives. I had worked in Africa where kids were so poor that they would wait outside a restaurant for the owner to come out, scrape the leftovers from his customers' plates into the communal bowl that they were holding, and then collectively share the discarded food among themselves. The kids on my unit at Lutheran Hospital were healthy-looking kids who for the most part came from families where their needs were taken care of, and yet they were in the hospital because of severe depression, eating disorders, schizophrenia and related mental health issues.

I would do programs for them that I thought would make them see how lucky they were to have their physical abilities, to walk, to see, to hear, and to have opportunities in life that people I knew, especially from Africa, never had and might never have. That is how unaware and ill-prepared I was for this job. It was only after working at the hospital, talking to the psychiatrists, psychologists, teachers and aides about the real struggles that these patients were experiencing, that I began to understand that mental illness is real and terribly debilitating. As I began to gain some knowledge and insight about mental illnesses, I did a much better job.

I learned something else about myself in the year or so that I worked at Lutheran. I had biases. I remember one evening when the ambulance arrived at the hospital with a middle-aged woman named Ida, who was about 5' tall and weighed about 200 lbs. She was in full-blown mania. She was screaming a great deal of profanity and threatened to kill the staff. The expletives continued non-stop until Ida was maneuvered into a padded room at the end of the hallway and the door was locked. Inside the padded room, Ida continued to vent. There was a window in the door, and I could see Ida's face from her nose up and her fingers clinging to the sides of the window as she kicked and screamed in vain. Eventually she more or less collapsed from fatigue.

I thought that this woman would challenge the best efforts of the psychiatrists on duty at that time. Fortunately for Ida, the doctors knew their stuff. They knew what her diagnosis was, and they quickly developed a medical treatment plan for her that would bring her back to reality. After about a week and a consistent drug regimen, Ida started to come back to earth. She was a sweet lady and had a great sense of humor. Now here's where my "don't judge a book by its cover" bias came into play. I imagined Ida had average intelligence at best. I don't think I was condescending to Ida, but I when I spoke with her it was out of a necessity to be nice and help her through her time in the hospital until she could be released back into the community. I remember one afternoon I went into the community room where everyone was smoking and watching television.

I walked into the room, and Ida was sitting with an older lady who I believe was suffering from a mild dementia. I was in my "therapeutic recreation" mode. I asked Ida and her companion if they'd like to play a game of Scrabble. The older lady said that she would like to play. I was a bit concerned about Ida. I was wondering if she even knew how to play Scrabble. Ida was smoking her cigarette intently. She looked up at me and said, "Sure, I'll play." I set the board for the three of us. I figured I'd humor both of them. We started the game and I put down the simplest word I could think of. The older lady was not wowing us with the words she laid down, but she was in the game. Ida, on the other hand, was playing the game as I was. She would take a puff on her cigarette, eye me up and put a word down that would mildly surprise me, but I figured it was a fluke. The game progressed towards the end. The older lady had most certainly given it her best, but she was behind by quite a bit.

Now, I can sometimes get a bit competitive, even under these circumstances. I was ahead of Ida, but not by much. It was my turn, and I laid down a word that put me ahead of Ida by probably 50 points. Ida took several more puffs of her cigarette, eyed me up and studied the board. She repeated these actions several times before I said, "Alright, Ida, what do you have?" Ida slowly finished flipping the last ash from her cigarette onto the floor and began methodically putting down her letters. I don't remember what the word was or how it connected to other words, but when I finished counting, she had accumulated 128 points! She killed me. She looked up from the board, made eye contact with me and began laughing her head off. She knew that I had dismissed her as not being that smart. I never made that mistake again.

## Temporary Career Change

I left the Lutheran Hospital in 1982 after about a year. It really was a valuable experience, but the mental health field was not in my future. During the time that I had worked at Lutheran, I got back into wheelchair basketball. I started coaching the Ravens wheelchair basketball team again. At that time wheelchair basketball provided an opportunity to play for only a limited number of players. There were no other options for players who did not make the Ravens. There was only one team, and if you didn't make it, you had to come to games and watch from the sidelines.

Sometime in 1982 I talked with one of the Ravens star players, Jimmy Leatherman, who had a double-leg amputation. Jimmy made contact with an owner of Abbey Medical, a regional medical supply company, about sponsoring a team. Jimmy was an administrator at the Social Security Administration, which was right down the street from Abbey Medical. He introduced me to the supervisor at the Abbey location. We got to talking about wheelchair sports as well as my involvement; he needed someone in his store to help with sales, and he offered me a job with the company. I mean, after all, I did have a B.S. degree in Business Management (with an emphasis on "B.S."). I left Lutheran Hospital and began a brief career in durable medical supply sales. The company folded about one year after I started. I'm not sure if it was because of my business management acumen or the lack thereof, but in that year, I had made some other contacts and wound up with a job at B.T. Smith Medical on North and Howard Streets in Baltimore City.

During this time with Abbey Medical, Jimmy and I formed the Baltimore Wheelchair Athletic Club, Inc. which became the second team in Baltimore and provided athletes with disabilities another team option. The program was successful and operated for over a decade. The players from this program also became part of my life and I've kept in touch with them over the years as I have the Ravens players. They too are survivors. I'd like to think that I played an important part in their lives but really, it's like all of the other people whom I have met. It's always been a mutually beneficial relationship.

I started my new job at B.T. Smith Medical at the end of 1983 and worked there until 1989, which amazes me as I write this. Gil Cohen, one of the owners, was the person who hired me, and he was a really nice guy who also supported my wheelchair basketball program. I've always been appreciative of his support in both my job and my wheel-chair basketball team during these years.

B.T. Smith Medical was an unusual place to work. At some point during my tenure there, they purchased an old funeral home adjacent to their warehouse building on the corner of North Avenue and Howard Street in West Baltimore. My office was relocated to the embalming room in the basement of the building. When I moved my office in there, there were still scalpels and related tools for preparing their customers for the afterlife. I never used any of the tools on anybody, but I did manage to sell a lot of medical equipment. Sometime in the 90's B.T. Smith moved its business, but the old and incredibly ugly building is still there, and on rare occasions when I'm driving through that area of West Baltimore I'll see the building, and it brings back a lot of good and some bizarre memories. I didn't dislike my job there, but it's not what I wanted to do for the rest of my life.

One moment that stands out during that time was listening one day to the office radio and hearing that Len Bias of the University of Maryland had died early that morning from a suspected drug overdose. That news shocked not only everyone in the office but everyone in the entire country. Bias had been chosen as a number one draft pick in the NBA lottery by the Boston Celtics. He was an absolutely incredible basketball player, and this news stunned everyone. It really was one of those "Kennedy assassination" moments. I just couldn't fathom that happening. People still talk about Bias's death in one of those "Where were you when Len Bias died?" kind of conversations.

## Career Change for Cass

I mentioned that Cass had gone to work for the V.A. Hospital at Fort Howard in Dundalk in 1982. She did an incredible job there. Her primary clientele were disabled World War II veterans. They all had chronic, life-changing disabilities that necessitated their living at Fort Howard to manage their health problems. Cass gave these men purpose. They would have a craft project building a dollhouse and then they'd raffle the completed structure, and the proceeds would go for parties at the facility. Cass, who was a deft card player, organized pinochle tournaments that these guys lived for. She organized a tournament against a group of disabled veterans from Perry Hall Veterans Hospital in Harford County, drove the bus her team was on and coordinated the on-site games. Her guys crushed it. They were so thrilled. Just to be recognized for doing something well in their condition raised their expectations, and that was what it was all about.

Cass did two more life-changing things in the 80's. In 1984 she had our first daughter Kate while working at Fort Howard. She didn't have Kate on the job, mind you, but she was still working there; but having said that, Cass could've had Kate at work and still have finished her shift. In 1986, she applied for and was hired her dream job as Executive Director of the Alzheimer's Association in Maryland. The organization had an annual budget of $50,000, and her starting salary was $400.00 a month. Cass had worked with a number of patients at the VA Medical Center who had dementia, and she was fascinated by this population. She was well aware of the lack of services and treatments for those impacted by Alzheimer's disease and related disorders and their families, and she was confident she could make a difference. Cass was the first staff person hired by this young nonprofit entirely run by volunteers. When she retired after 35 years in 2020, and the organization now had a $5 million annual budget a staff of over 25 employees and three offices in Maryland. During those years thousands of people with Alzheimer's and their families benefited immeasurably from the efforts of Cass, her staff and board members.

Also, in 1986 our second daughter Emma was born, and our son Michael was born in 1990. Those six years between 1984 and 1990 were busy years. Phew! During those years I felt like I was making a contribution to the family and that I was supportive of Cass. In retrospect, Cass did it all. As I reflect back, I realized how hard Cass worked for our family. She was nothing short of amazing during the

80's, and in the present for that matter. but I wish I had been a better contributor during those years. In the mid-2000's, I think I was starting to get there. When I'm 90 I hope to be able to say, "I was a help along the way."

## My Dream Job

My involvement with wheelchair basketball had continued during the time that I worked selling wheelchairs and crutches at B.T. Smith Medical. It was nice having something that I enjoyed outside of my job. For those of you who have trudged through this lengthy narrative, you may remember my mentioning a gentleman named Ralph W. Jones, Jr., the person responsible for my obtaining a Master's Degree in Urban Recreation at the University of Baltimore back in 1977. I had maintained a relationship with Ralph from my time in the 70's. In 1989 Ralph was selected by then Baltimore City Mayor Kurt Schmoke to be the Director of Recreation and Parks for the City of Baltimore. One of Ralph's first outreaches was to me to see If I would be interested in being the Director of Therapeutic Recreation in his Department. I would be making a salary that at the time seemed huge to me, along with the benefits that came with a government job, but more importantly I would be taking a position that was meant for me. I would be able to expand wheelchair sports opportunities and provide innovative adapted recreation programs for children and adults with disabilities who lived in Baltimore City. My time of selling durable medical products at B.T. Smith was quickly coming to a conclusion. My Business Management Degree would be retired. I was hired by the Department of Recreation and Parks, and I began my twenty-two-year career in therapeutic recreation in July of 1989.

This was a wonderful opportunity for me. The program that was in place at that time was a somewhat antiquated recreational model for children and adults with disabilities. The people who ran the program were well-intentioned and were incredibly nice people but seemed to have lacked the vision necessary to initiate meaningful program experiences that had actual positive measurable outcomes.

The program was housed in an industrial park in Dundalk at the very outskirts of Baltimore City. The building where programs were run and which housed my office was the old Fort Holabird Army Induction Center. The center was used as such until the end of the Vietnam War. My friend Tom Stough was inducted there. Tom, was about 6' 8" tall and had anticipated being turned down for the draft because of his height. He was indeed measured at 6' 8" tall and told to go home until, as Tom describes it, "A sergeant said, 'Let me re-measure him." He did so at 6' 7 ½" and Tom was off to Vietnam.

I started my recreation and parks career in June of 1989. My first experience was with Camp Variety. Every time I start writing I think of things that take me off course. Camp Variety got its name from a traveling variety show that was started in Pittsburgh in 1927 by a group of actors. At some point the show came to Baltimore, and the staff from the "Handicapped Recreation Program" (as it was known then) took a group of children and adults with disabilities to see the show. These participants evidently made such an impression on the showmen that they donated a van to the program with the condition that "Donated by the Variety Club" be written on its side. This donation was so appreciated by the staff and participants that it was decided that their new identifying name would be "The Variety Club."

I came to Camp Variety that summer after the six-week program had already begun. To my amazement there were 250 kids with disabilities on-site with every disability imaginable, but the common denominator for almost every camper was poverty. The site was about half an acre. It included a swimming pool that had been part of the Army's officers' club prior to the army leaving for parts unknown. The pool had a water pipe to feed water into the pool, and it was always gushing water.

When I asked what the deal was with this water pipe, I was told that it been that way for several summers because there was a crack in the pool, and in order to keep the water level up, it was necessary to run water constantly. Apparently, this problem had existed for several summers and the problem had not been rectified. The staff there assured me that regardless how the camp appeared to me, it was quite an upgrade from where the camp had been previously housed. I was told the story of Camp Variety prior to its Fort Holabird location. The first Camp Variety was held at a place called Fort Smallwood, a city-owned "rustic" park in Anne Arundel County. It was on the water, which increased my fear of where this story was headed.

Camp Variety began operating in the summer months in the 60's and 70's. There doesn't appear to be any historical record showing the exact year it began. The camp was situated next to the Patapsco River. In addition to kids with diagnosed disabilities, the camp served campers who were impoverished. During some summers where there were over 600 kids from Baltimore City who were bused to Camp Variety. There were no buildings at the camp except for a small building that was used as an office. Apparently, there were no bathrooms, but I have to think there were some-type of spot-a-pots indiscriminately positioned here and there—but I can't be sure. Fifteen to twenty buses were needed to transport these kids to and from the city. What happened when they got there and got off the bus I really don't know, but if you talk to adults today in Baltimore City who attended Camp Variety in those years, they have nothing but fond memories. If it rained while kids were at camp, the staff would herd the kids back onto the buses. If it rained really hard, with no chance of stopping, they would simply turn the buses around and take the campers back home. At the end of the day, I guess the one redeeming quality about the program as it existed was that it was free, but you got what you paid for.

There is one story about one particular summer day in the 70's at Camp Variety that astounded me. As the story was relayed to me, the campers finished their day and they had been herded back onto their buses for a return trip home to Baltimore City. Amazingly, someone discovered that there was a missing camper. All hell broke loose as the staff decided to spread out and scour the woods for the lost soul. Jerome McCardell, the recreation center director recounted to me how the incident evolved. Besides being a center director for kids and adults with disabilities, Jerome, an accomplished musician, worked nights as a drummer for a band on the infamous "Block" on Baltimore Street in Baltimore City and he had developed a core of friends and associates at the various strip clubs there. He knew that as many people as possible would be needed to find this missing kid. Now remember, this camp was located next to the Patapsco River in Anne Arundel County about 10 miles from the city. No call to my knowledge of the situation went out to authorities. The staff decided to take on the search and rescue mission themselves, probably fearing they would be fired if they couldn't locate the little guy. Jerome sent a bus to the strip club district in Baltimore City and recruited strippers to come down and join the search party. At the end of the day, I think they found the camper huddled up behind one of the bus seats sleeping. The strippers I'm told found the young camper so their own search and rescue mission was not in vain. They were transported back to the "Block" in time for their evening shift. All's well that ends well. I should note here too that on another occasion these strippers were also recruited by Jerome to do a "strip-a-thon" on a makeshift stage on Baltimore Street to raise money for the Camp Variety program. The club owners on the Block all agreed to this. I can only assume that in the end, some money was raised and Camp Variety got some publicity. If this event had been held in the 2000's, Jerome may have lost his job but he would have gone out in a Blaze (Starr) of glory.

Jerome McCardell was the Center Director at Camp Variety, and it was he who recounted some of the program history to me. He had been with the program since its inception in the late 60's. He was one of the nicest and most well-meaning people I have ever known. He was one of the most accepting people that I ever knew as well. A great staff person would gain Jerome's praise, but a terrible staff person would get equal billing, and in my limited experience with the program at that time, there were a reasonable number of staff in the latter category; however, the good staff were really good. Nonetheless, I had nothing but respect for Jerome.

It was my job to reconstruct Camp Variety to ensure that the kids who attended would be introduced to experiences that had some lasting impact on their lives. In defense of the people who came before me who put these programs together, they were well-meaning, nice people. How they pieced programs together or how they treated people came from their own experiences. The staff and volunteers in this program did the absolute best they could to provide the campers with memorable experiences. In addition, most of these staff workers were respectful of what I was trying to do to make the program better, or at the very least they tolerated me being there. Their acceptance meant a lot to me.

My other major concern for this program was safety, a problem that even my harshest critics could understand. There were just too many minor accidents that had occurred and too many more waiting to happen. My objective after that first summer was to move the program to a more appropriate location. It was not just inaccessible to participants but to staff and volunteers as well. One of the staff people, Corey Brooks, who was blind, navigated his way back to the remote location every day and it never seized to amaze me how he did so.

Corey was our "music coordinator." In 1989 I believe Corey was in his 20's. He was a really talented keyboard player, musician and exceptionally nice young man who had been totally blind since birth. He also had been involved with the Camp Variety program since he was two years old. To explain that, I'd have to write two more pages. We were still in the Fort Holabird location into the winter; in fact, we had to spend one more summer there. In the fall and winter months, Corey would come to work on a city bus, probably two or three buses from where he lived in West Baltimore. Every day he would get off the bus at Dundalk Avenue and walk back to our center, which was nearly a mile from where Corey got off the bus. Now, the fact that he was blind but could ride these buses to this final bus stop was in itself fascinating to me, but that he navigated this path to our center that only he knew never failed to blow me away.

In life we sometimes take things for granted; our abilities to be independent, our ability to hear, our ability to see. One day at work I had to go to the bathroom, and when I walked into the men's bathroom it was totally dark. I heard someone standing at the urinal peeing. I flicked on the light and was shocked to see Corey standing there at the urinal. I said, "Corey, what are you doing peeing in the dark?" He responded, "Mike—I'm blind." We both burst out laughing at the same time.

I have one more Corey and Jerome tale. Jerome informed me one day that he had received a call from someone representing a circus that was performing in Timonium in Baltimore County. They were offering free tickets for an afternoon performance that week; would Jerome be interested in bringing a group of participants from the Variety Club? Jerome loved these kinds of opportunities. On the other hand, I hated circuses. Jerome arranged to transport a large group of adults with disabilities to the event, and Corey was included in the mix. Jerome said that the circus performers were about halfway through the opening act when he noticed the person playing the organ appeared kind of wobbly. The next thing he knew, the organist who appeared to be really drunk, fell off the little stage where he was playing and was totally incapacitated. There came an announcement over the P.A. system asking, "Does anybody here play the organ?" Without blinking an eye, Jerome stood up and volunteered Corey's services. The circus people were skeptical but desperate. After a brief hesitation they agreed to give Corey a shot. Jerome sat beside him and gave him cues as to when to play the "circus music." Corey did such a great job that the representatives of the circus asked him to stay and play for the evening performance, but Corey had to decline. It was one thing to take three buses to work every morning but it was another to navigate your way home from the circus.

In the years since these stories occurred both Jerome and Corey have passed on. They were both incredibly nice people and remarkable musicians. They were both important fixtures in my life and in the lives of the people whom they served.

## A Sad Moment in Time

A terribly sad event occurred for me and for the Department of Recreation and Parks in 1990. My dear friend and mentor Ralph W. Jones, Jr., unexpectedly suffered a massive heart attack and died in transit to the hospital. Ralph had a beautiful wife and just the nicest young sons. It was a tragedy and huge loss for his family, for me and for all who knew him from Recreation and Parks, and for the many students and colleagues he had known over the years from Morgan State University and the University of Baltimore.

Ralph was the finest Director of Recreation and Parks in its history as far as I'm concerned. His passion was recreation and the value it had in people's lives. He loved going to a community recreation center and seeing children learning chess, involved in a dance class or participating in a pick-up game of basketball. This would bring him tremendous joy because he knew these kids were involved in a constructive activity that taught teaching life skills that could be beneficial to them in later life. Ralph was simply a caring, compassionate person who valued everyone's life. I have missed him over the years. I will always remember him for the contribution that he made to so many people's lives, including mine.

## Our Move to Brooklyn

The City of Baltimore agreed that we needed to move to a better location for the Therapeutic Recreation Division programs. We investigated various facilities, some of which were more dilapidated and inaccessible than Fort Holabird, but there were some with potential. We finally settled on the Farring-Baybrook Recreation Center in the Brooklyn neighborhood in South Baltimore.

Our program came to Farring-Baybrook with the majority of my year-round staff, which included my Center Director, Recreation Leader and several part-time Recreation Assistants. My Recreation Leader Spencer Crowder and his wife Jackie ("Salt of the earth" is the best description of this lady} had been with the program for a few years prior to my coming on board. Spencer was disabled. He was nearly blind but still visually functional for the lack of a better description. Spencer also was a single leg amputee. I had known Spencer prior to my getting the job with City. Spencer participated on one of the wheelchair basketball teams that I was involved with in the 70's and 80's. Bob Ardinger, one of the few legitimately good players who I coached, had a nickname for everyone, and his nickname for Spencer was "Peepers."

"Peepers," or Spencer, was a sort of counselor for a small group of adults with developmental disabilities who came to our program in Dundalk and who stayed with the program when we moved to Brooklyn. Spence had his limitations, but he really looked out for and protected this young to middle-aged group of folks with disabilities. We took day trips with this group to sports-related venues—bowling alleys, skating arenas, etc.—and occasionally on shopping trips to the mall. If any of the program participants had issues or created problems, it was always Spencer who stepped in to resolve the problems. We had one participant who was on the autism spectrum who loved magazines and when the group would go to a mall, this one magazine-loving guy would go into a grocery store or pharmacy and pick out magazines that he liked. Now, he never had money to pay for the magazines and would leave without paying. It was always Spencer's job to guide this person back into the store, let the store manager know that the "would be buyer" had some issues and the magazines were returned to their racks.

Spencer died in 2019. He is fondly remembered by those who knew him well.

The Farring-Baybrook Recreation Center was an upgrade from our Dundalk site, but there was a lot of work to be done. During the 90's I was able to have a number of renovations made that benefited our program as well as the community programs. I was able to get funding to create a gym by raising the ceiling in what had been a large community room. I found the funding to change three underused tennis courts in the park adjacent to the building into a wheelchair softball field. Ultimately by the early 2000's the building and grounds had been renovated to meet Americans with Disability Act standards. A state-of-the-art handicapped accessible playground was added as well as three lighted bocce courts. I did all of this through grants, begging and being conveniently obsequious when all else failed.

Our newly reconfigured gym enabled me to offer wheelchair basketball at the facility. The Metro Wheelchair Basketball League for many years offered all players an opportunity to play in a competitive league twice a week. This was a recreational league where all players regardless of their disability had an opportunity to participate in basketball. I received a grant that allowed me to purchase about a dozen sports wheelchairs that could be used by all participants for the games. At that time wheelchairs that were designed for that purpose cost about $3,000 and were generally not approved for people with physical disabilities by their health insurance policies. They were cost-prohibitive for the vast majority of players, especially players from impoverished neighborhoods in the city.

I conducted the league as a competitive league. The games had referees, and we had basketball seasons that would cover most of the winter months, including play-offs and championships. We even sold hot dogs, candy bars, popcorn and sodas out of our gym kitchen to make the games like they would be if conducted in an able-bodied basketball league. I also stipulated that the league be open to able-bodied players. I did this for a several reasons. First, siblings and friends many times provided transportation for the players, and when they got to the center found themselves trying out the sports wheelchairs and loving the experience; and second, it assured them that they could play. The last reason was that we would consistently have enough players to have a viable league. The players with disabilities had no problems with the concept, and really, they were the superior players. Their personal experiences of being in wheelchairs and knowing how to handle them gave them an advantage on the court.

In addition to having competitive players (players who also played on sanctioned National Wheelchair Basketball Association teams), we had players whose disabilities were so limiting that they would never be able to play on a competitive level. All players played. That was the rule, and it was up to the skilled players to be creative in how they used their more disabled teammates. The concept worked well. The games became competitive enough that winning was the objective. That was to be expected, but when a more severely disabled player somehow scored a basket, the whole gym would go wild. "Feel-good moments" were more than acceptable in the Metro League. There was no condescension involved, just an appreciation for players maximizing their abilities. We raised these players expectations.

Camp Variety was transplanted from Dundalk to Brooklyn, but the model had significantly changed. The first thing that I did was to cut the number of campers who attended Camp Variety. It wasn't my intention to lessen the opportunities for kids to attend camp, but I had to divide the camp into shorter sessions; groups of campers based on age and disability would come for shorter times, but the time they spent there would be safe and they would receive positive attention from staff. Programs would be adapted to meet their special needs based on their individual disabilities.

I was able to convince our department that the staff I needed would have responsibilities that were far greater than other summer camp programs, and to attract a better staff I would need more money in our budget. Higher salaries enabled me to recruit more college students, many of whom were students in human service-related curriculums at their respective colleges. I also hired a number of young people from the Brooklyn community and that helped to develop good relations with the community.

I planned program trips that kids with disabilities in the city were unlikely to have had: trips on the newly opened light rail system from one end of the line to the other; a trip to the BWI Airport to watch the passenger planes come in at almost eye level and where the campers made and displayed a large paper banner that read, "Camp Variety welcomes you to Baltimore!" Victor West whom I had known as camper in the 70's at Camp Greentop was my arts and crafts director at Camp Variety directed the banner making as well as our camp crafts program.

Victor also provided a safe space in his craft room for kids with behavior disorders. Victor was sort of an imposing kind of guy. He demanded quiet in his area when crafts were in session. All it took for the kids with behavior issues to behave was a slam on the table from Victor's fist. That doesn't sound very therapeutic but we had neither the space nor the money to create any other options. The kids knew Victor would not tolerate bad behavior so kids who were predisposed to such behavior would come in, sit down and do their projects knowing that they would be safe from other kids with similar issues from getting into arguments with them.

We hiked and took fishing trips in state parks, went canoeing and horseback riding, had trips to the Top of the World Trade Center in Baltimore, museums and the National Aquarium. One of my favorite trips was to the Carrie Murray Nature Center in Leakin Park in Baltimore City. Named for the mother of Oriole baseball Hall-of-Famer, Eddie Murray, who provided the funding, the center is one those very hidden gems in Baltimore City.

Here is the reason why I loved this place. My favorite fiction author of all time is Tom Robbins. For me, he is just one of the most creatively funny writers, and what makes his books hilarious is that once wrapped up in one of his stories, they become almost believable. My absolute favorite book by him is *Another Roadside Attraction*. At the beginning of the book, he introduces a couple of exotic characters, John Paul Ziller and Amanda who operate this off the beaten path roadside zoo of sorts with an assortment of animals and insects not typically found in a conventional zoo. Carrie Murray Nature is about as close as you can get to "Another Roadside Attraction." Corinne Parks the Director at that time, is Amanda. The nature center's purpose was to rescue wild birds like hawks, eagles and owls who had suffered injuries and try to rehab them and return them to their natural environments. If they couldn't be rehabbed, they would be housed at the nature center, kept in a safe and appropriate habitat and be available for viewing by Baltimore City school children. It was an environmental education center. Over time, for reasons unknown to everyone except Corinne, she started adopting tropical exotic birds like cockatoos who would outlive their owners. When you visited the center, the birds would start "shouting out" crazy words and phrases that Corinne taught them. In addition, there were snakes, turtles, iguanas (they too were adoptees) and the aforementioned indigenous wild birds. The center also had section for bizarre insects. The center was located in the middle of Leakin Park, the second largest woodland park in the United States. The sign for the Carrie Murray Center was located on a winding two-lane road leading into West Baltimore and the sign itself, although a beautifully painted sign was simply a blur for anyone driving by. Aside from all of the above, the center and park were beautiful. We would take kids from Camp Variety there for all sorts of adventures and it was both an educational and memorable experience.

We were able to do all of these programs and trips from the revenue that was generated from privately-donated camperships for the majority of the campers who attended Camp Variety. Bias aside, we had the best summer programs of any recreation center in Baltimore City. I'm quite sure that the campers who attended camp in the 90's and the 2000's have great memories of their experiences there; at least, those were my intentions.

## Shameless Nepotisim

The other important year-round staff that I added were "the Gardner family." Mary Gardner was a resident of the Brooklyn community and a strong advocate for those who lived in Brooklyn. She was a teacher's aide at that time at the elementary school adjacent to the recreation center and volunteered her spare time at the center with the kids from the Brooklyn neighborhood. Everyone knew and respected her. I needed part-time staff for my year-round programs, and she asked if she could apply. She did and I hired her. She had three daughters and two sons and a cornucopia of nieces, nephews and grandchildren, all of whom lived in the neighborhood. My staff objective (as previously stated for my summer camp program) was to hire people with college degrees in Therapeutic Recreation and begin to create a real therapeutic model for the city; however, there never were enough funds to do so during my tenure with the Department of Recreation and Parks, so I had to build as productive a staff as I could with what was available. Mary and her family were available.

Mary and her family members were simply tough-minded survivors. None of them had a college degree, but all were incredibly smart, both intellectually and streetwise. The family often had serious money problems and tortuous personal relationships. They were also incredibly loyal to one another no matter what and would rally around to rectify any problems that occurred within the family and try to ease the pain. They belonged to one of the few white families that lived in the Brooklyn neighborhood of South Baltimore, where my office was located for twenty years. If you've ever seen the Netflix series "Shameless" well, I'm thinking they may have based the series on Mary's family.

You had to be tough to grow up in Brooklyn. People in that community were survivors. Sadly, some people did not survive. During that time there were probably fifteen to twenty young people that I knew relatively well who were murdered in that neighborhood, and drug addiction was and is rife, and yet life went on. Among those young people who died were Mary Gardner's grandson, Aaron Shipley and one of his best friends Isaiah Drummond. They both fell victim to the streets of South Baltimore between 2019 and 2021. Both of these young men were about 30 years old. Aaron and Isaiah were two of the nicest, caring young people that I knew during the time I worked in Brooklyn. I wanted to include them in my book to remember them. Brooklyn was, as I have described, an impoverished, drug infested community but there were many incredibly nice people who continue to this day to do the best that they can to survive in the neighborhood. Aaron and Isaiah's lives were cut short, they made a positive impact on the people in the community and that will be their legacy.

In the summers when I worked in Brooklyn, I was able to hire all of Mary's kids, grandchildren, nieces and nephews at one time or another because they all had different last names. I can't quite explain why that was but because they had different last names, no one questioned who they were related to. Now, you might say this appears to border on nepotism and you would probably be right, but her family members were kind, compassionate employees who always had the best interests of our campers in mind, and I love survivors. Mary eventually was promoted to a full-time position with our division, and she became an integral part of the Therapeutic Recreation Department. The one quality which can't be measured that made her special was being a "nurturer," as were her children. When you have kids who come from terrible backgrounds, have severe self-esteem problems and want to fight the world in retaliation for the hand they were dealt, Mary was "The Man." She made kids and adults with these issues feel special, and that may have made all of my programs work far better perhaps than if I had been able to hire trained Therapeutic Recreation Specialists.

Speaking of "nepotism," to the casual observer it might appear that I too was "a little" guilty of the practice. From the time my own kids Kate, Emma and Michael were old enough, I would take them with me to camp as campers every summer from the mid-90's to the 2000's until they graduated from high school; and when they were old enough, I hired them as staff. I know to the casual observer this does not seem quite right, but personal bias aside, they were all among the best summer staff that I ever had. I also may have hired my nieces and nephews and a few of their friends, and my sister-in-law Trish was our camp nurse. She too was the best nurse that we ever had at camp. This of course would've been my justification had anyone questioned my personnel decisions, and I'm sure that those in power would've said, "Yes, Mr. Naugle, this seems perfectly acceptable."

## Chicago Ball

During the summer months, in addition to Camp Variety, in the evenings we had wheelchair softball practices and games at Farring-Brook's wheelchair softball field which as I noted earlier had been tennis courts. Wheelchair softball in and of itself is not so different from able-bodied softball except for the ball which is called a "Chicago

Ball". It has a 16" circumference and it's used in able-bodied recreational leagues in Chicago. It's not as hard as a conventional softball and you can catch it with without a glove. This adapts well to wheelchair softball because you can't push a chair and wear a baseball glove at the same time.

We had a very successful program. I will leave it at that but I did want to mention one special player who meant a lot to me as well as the other players in the program. He was a "super quad" which means he was classified as a quadriplegic for the game of wheelchair softball. His name was Claude Hall. Claude to this day was one of my favorite wheelchair athletes and people. I would be remiss and Claude would be mad at me if I didn't mention also that he was a really good wheelchair basketball player. Claude died unexpectedly in 2019. He had a congenital disability that affected all four of his limbs. He had extremely short legs, one arm that was functional but had limited use and the other arm that was as powerful as an able-bodied weight-lifter. He could smack the crap out of a softball. He was probably the most valuable player the team had because of his classification and because of his one-arm power. He was responsible for winning a lot of wheelchair softball games for his Baltimore team in the nineties. Claude's biggest attribute though was as an ambassador for wheelchair sports. He was a shining example of an athlete who maximized his abilities and the relationships that he made over the years with so many other wheelchair athletes and everyone who knew him were relationships of love and respect. Claude will be remembered by many for years to come.

## Moving to Mt. Airy

In 1995 our family moved to Mt. Airy, Maryland. This was a difficult move for all of us. Cass had grown up in Locust Point, I had lived there for almost twenty-five years, and our kids who were eleven, nine and five had spent their early years in the "Point." It was a wonderful time, but my parents were getting older, and we wanted to live in a more central location in Maryland that was accessible to both of our sets of parents, and we wanted our children to have an opportunity to be in a really good public school system. Mt. Airy seemed to fill the bill. When we moved to Mt. Airy, the population was between 5,000 and 6,000 residents. Now, almost twenty-six years later, the population is between 12,000 and 15,000.

Our kids were not happy initially, but we found a house with a pool and great backyard that includes county land that we use and maintain for family gatherings and parties. That made the move a bit more tolerable for them. Every year for the past quarter of a century we have hosted a family and friends 4th of July party. It's not uncommon to have 75 or 80 guests. The guests include our extended family and friends from both Cass and childhood, friends from our college and Peace Corps years and friends with whom we worked in our careers. I think at the end of the day, these parties will be our legacy. It was a good move.

## Silver Anniversary but Watch Your Pockets

In 1997 Cass and I celebrated our 25th wedding anniversary with a trip back to Paris. Looking back, we can't remember who took care of our kids during that time. We took kind of an economy trip. Maybe we had to pay somebody a whole lot of money to look after our children. It turned out to be a great trip, so apparently, we didn't have any guilt feelings associated with leaving the kids behind.

We stayed in a suburban area of Paris called Asnieres-sur-Seine, an area about 8 kilometers northwest of Paris, and we had to take a short train ride in and out of Paris each day, which was interesting. There were working-class people taking this train, packed in with us tourists from America. It was interesting seeing Paris from that perspective.

Another unexpected perspective were the Romani or Roma people. Our proximity to train stations a couple times a day brought us in close contact with these wayfarers. I have expounded upon how important sympathy and empathy are when exposed to people of different backgrounds, especially people who, for whatever reason didn't get a fair shake in life. Whether it be beggars in Africa or homeless people in our cities in America, I always feel a sense of both sadness and guilt, and if I have some money to offer, I do. However, the Roma tested my guilt, sympathy and compassion to the max. In the train stations in Paris, they were everywhere, and when you thought you had avoided them, they'd pop up unexpectedly just after you purchased your morning coffee and pastry at a kiosk in the middle of the station. I'd be accosted by these innocent young girls with big brown eyes, who were dressed in well-worn, tattered brownish clothing. Now generally, when I give a hand-out, I don't expect the recipient to give me a "God bless you, sir" response. I have never had to deal with the issues that have caused people to beg for money for their very existence. If I have some discretionary money to give, I give it, and how the recipients use it is up to them.

When one these young women accosts me and asks for money for food, my initial reaction to their plight is to give them some money, but here's the problem. Let's say I give a Roma woman two Euros, which is equivalent to about three or four dollars. That seems like a reasonable donation to me, but not to the Roma woman. She said, "Please sir, this is not enough, could you give me more?" While I was contemplating what to do next, other young women gathered around me assessing how they might pick-pocket some item or money precariously exposed among my clothes or backpack. I have to give them credit for being so good at their craft, but they tend to give people who truly need a hand-out a bad name.

Cass and I loved our second time in Paris. We saw things we missed the first time around and revisited the places that gave us such joy when we were last there in 1981. One of the tourist destinations that eluded our inspection twenty-five years earlier was the Rodin Museum. Cass had studied the works of Rodin in school, and the museum was on our to-do list. She absolutely loved it and pointed out Rodin's artistry to me. I listened and observed and thought to myself, "His works are pretty good."

## End of a Life Well Lived

On November 5, 1999, Jack died. He was 80 years old. I got a call from Hazel saying that Jack was in the hospital and was not doing well. By the time I got to the Washington County Hospital in Hagerstown, he was gone. I was very lucky to have had him in my life for 52 years. He did so much for me, and I never took the time to tell him how much I appreciated him. While I wish I had taken advantage of the many things he attempted to teach me, the one lasting thing that he did teach me that stuck was empathy for others.

There were two simple stories that I remember when I talked with him in later life which illustrate the gift that he passed on to me. The first is when he was a kid growing up in Chambersburg. Jack befriended a deaf boy his age who lived on a small farm behind the house he grew up in on Center Street. Jack and his brothers grew up during the Depression. I never got the idea that lack of food was a problem, but he and his brothers did a fair amount of hunting in the area, and it wasn't for sport; it was for an evening meal. On one such outing he happened upon this boy who was his age, and he quickly realized that he was deaf. Instead of being uncomfortable because of not being able to communicate verbally, he just started gesturing to his new acquaintance, who also gestured, and they established communication. They remained childhood friends, which I can't help but think was a blessing in particular for the boy who was deaf, but also for Jack. I'm sure they both benefited from this relationship.

The other story that has stayed with me is about an experience Jack had on the railroad. The Western Maryland Railroad had many job destinations for its train crews, among which was the Cumberland run to Cumberland, Maryland. The train would stop periodically in different towns along the way. One such town was Hancock, Maryland. The crew would usually get off the train there to eat lunch at a local roadside restaurant. On one such lunch break, Jack noticed a Black man and his family parked in front of the restaurant. He observed the man get out of his car and walk to the rear of the restaurant and then he returned with a bag of lunches for his family. The man was not allowed to come into the restaurant either by himself or with his family because of their race. Jack said that he imagined his own family being turned down from entering that restaurant and what that would do to them. He never ate at that restaurant again. While that story may not have affected the business at that restaurant, it affected me, and I have always tried to follow Jack's example. I hope have been able to pass some of his traits on to my own children.

## Getting "Hip" in my Old Age

The other life-altering experience that I had in 1999 was getting a new hip. All of that jumping had taken a toll on my left leg. I was old before my time (but still a legend in my own mind). I could hardly walk, but the surgical procedure enabled me to regain my mobility. My jumping days were behind me, mind you, but the thing that a new hip gave me was an opportunity to get back into playing basketball—wheelchair basketball. As you're aware after trudging through this literary gem, I had been involved for years as a coach for a wheelchair basketball team. The primary qualification to play wheelchair basketball competitively was that you had to have a permanent lower-limb physical disability that would significantly limit your ability to play able-bodied sports. At age 52 I became a wheelchair basketball point forward. A new career was in my future but more on that later.

## Where Were You When?

My mind always tends to fade in and out as I'm trying to maintain a chronological order of things. This is another one of those "Where were you when this happened?" years. On September 11, 2001, I was driving to work on Route 100 in Howard County, Maryland, listening to Tony Kornheiser's program on ESPN Radio station 980. Tony Kornheiser is my favorite sports analyst. He was a great sports journalist for *The Washington Post* as well, and I always enjoyed reading his articles. His sarcastic sense of humor keeps sports in proper perspective.

As I listened to Tony, he said to one of his on-air partners, "Here's something interesting that just came in. A plane has hit the World Trade Center in New York City. What a bizarre thing. I wonder what kind of plane. I guess it was a small plane. I really don't know." Then the report revealed that it was a passenger plane, and that changed the tone of the on-air conversation. You could hear the shock in Tony's now shaky voice as well as his colleague's.

I couldn't fathom what was happening. When I got to work, my staff had the television on, watching in horror what was transpiring. We saw the second plane hit and ultimately witnessed the collapse of the World Trade Center. The aftermath of this terrible act of terrorism included the deaths of so many people and remains indelibly ingrained in my mind. I still cannot believe that such an absolute tragedy occurred on that day. There are incidents like this, along with the Kennedy assassination, the terrible explosion of the Challenger Space Shuttle in 1986, and the death of Len Bias in June of 1986, that shock one into the reality of the fragility of the world in which we live. The pandemic of 2020 is certainly in this same category of tragic events, as we continue to deal with it.

## No Dunking Allowed

Now back to basketball. Basketball is life, after all. When I say I became a wheelchair basketball player, I really didn't start playing competitively until 2004. Having played in practices for thirty years, transitioning to a wheelchair was not an issue. Actually, playing in a competitive game gave me an even greater appreciation of how challenging the game can be. In 2005 I played for the Baltimore Ravens wheelchair basketball team. Ed Diggs, my long-time friend, Ravens coach and future National Wheelchair Basketball Association Hall-of-Fame member, had co-erced me into playing the previous year, and in 2005 we qualified for the National Wheelchair Basketball Association Division III National Tournament in Illinois. Now, let me say that as a then 58-year-old wheelchair basketball player, I was nowhere near the oldest player in the tournament. As I'm sitting here writing this, there are wheelchair basketball players that I knew starting out in the game as a coach in 1970 who are still playing competitive wheelchair basketball—not par-ticularly well, mind you, but they're out there. I am not one of them.

In March of 2005, I packed up my 1999 Ford Ranger pick-up truck with sports wheelchairs as well as Ron Shaffer, a Class 1 player, and we headed to Illinois for the National Division III Tournament. I mentioned Ron's player classification. In wheelchair basketball your physical abili-ties are assessed by certified physical therapists. Class 1's are the most disabled players and generally have higher thoracic spinal cord injuries. Their paralysis extends from their chest area down. Class 2's in most cases are players with lower thoracic spinal column injuries, and while they can be ambulatory or non-ambulatory, their paralysis is generally from the waist down. Class 3's are the least disabled. Class 3's could include players with partial lower extremity spinal cord injuries, ampu-tees and players like myself (thankfully there is no mental component involved in the classification process) with injuries that would perma-nently prevent them from competing in able-bodied basketball (which, at 74 I still do regardless).

Teams are allowed to have 12 points on the floor at one time. (Stay with me here.) The objective of wheelchair basketball is to enable the most disabled players to play basketball. You can have any combination of players on the court, but only three Class 3's can play at one time. Three 3's, one Class 2 and one Class 1 adds up to 12 points. You can have less than 12 points but no more. In theory you could have five Class 1's playing at one time

There were two or three other players who drove, driving themselves as well as teammates and equipment on this fourteen-hour road trip. Ron, who was riding with me, worked hard over the years and became a very good wheelchair basketball player. He also had a good sense of humor, which was essential on this grueling drive. We pretty much drove straight through except to stop several times at Ron's favorite restaurant, Cracker Barrel, or to stop so for bathroom breaks. When Ron talked about the chicken-fried steak at Cracker Barrel, he described it like one would describe fine French cuisine. "I'm telling you, Mike, it's the best thing you've ever tasted." I had never frequented a Cracker Barrel Restaurant before, but I became quite familiar with them on this trip. The chicken-fried steak was good, but that along with their famous chocolate brownie with ice cream would kill you if you ate that meal more than once a month.

Now let me get to the tournament. I believe there were sixteen teams from all over the country in the competition. It was a double-elimination tournament, so you could lose a game and still have a chance to move on. The first day we lost one of three games, but that kept us in a consolation bracket with a chance to move on the next day. I don't know what occurred the next day in terms of bracketing, but we won our first game, which put us back into the winner's bracket. We then started another game and won, and what transpired from there still astounds me. We had to play five consecutive games. Games are set up with two twenty-minute halves just like the N.C.A.A., so with time-outs and half-times each game would take approximately two hours to complete. We played for ten straight hours before losing in the final game that would have put us into the championship. We finished in 3rd place. Gino Wilson (about whom I could write another book) and I had shared one of those large packs of Juicy Fruit Gum during the duration of these marathon games. When we finished, we both realized at the same time that the gum we had been chewing had turned to powder. That's how dehydrated we were. We both laughed our heads off at this phenomenon. Our hands took weeks to heal completely. I retired from wheelchair basketball after that tournament. The following year in 2006 the Ravens won the championship. I may have been holding them back.

## League of Dreams

I am going to backtrack a bit here so I can mention a couple of other programs that I started in the early 2000's that had some positive impact. The first is the League of Dreams Baseball Program. Frank Kolarek, a former professional baseball player with the Oakland A's organization, had contacted our director's office about starting a baseball program for kids with disabilities, and the director put Frank in contact with me. When we met, we decided that in order for the program to have a chance to succeed, we should take a regional approach and include Baltimore County Recreation and Parks as well.

Baltimore County during the 90's had built a regulation macadam wheelchair softball field just outside of the Baltimore beltway. Despite their best efforts, the field was underused and they too were looking for programs that would provide more opportunities for people with disabilities, especially kids with disabilities. I suggested we use the county field, and I would promote the program for families of children with disabilities in Baltimore City and do what I could do to help coordinate the program. Frank, the Director and Founder of the League of Dreams had the baseball expertise and also had worked for Special

Olympics International, so he knew how to adapt the ability levels of the kids to best include them and create positive learning experiences. I volunteered to find the funding for team shirts and hats, buy refreshments for the kids and be there as an assistant coach.

The first year we had between twenty and thirty kids aged six to twenty-one with every disability imaginable. Players having the basic physical skills to play baseball were personally instructed in a way that would help to improve their skill level. The players who had a severe disability that required rolling a ball to them, having them pick the ball up and throw back in your direction would receive personal instruction on how to do this better. If a ball with a bell in it was needed for a player who was blind, that ball was provided, and that player was coached to improve his or her skill level. The parents of these kids were so incredibly appreciative. Higher-functioning kids were blended in with lower-functioning kids for games, and you would have thought it was a regular Little League game. The League of Dreams is still in operation in 2021, and it started with that program.

## The Variety Children's Theatre and Dance Project

The program that I was most proud of was the Variety Children's Theatre Project. Now, if you have actually read my story from the beginning, you will recall how much I hated musicals when I was young, but this program did not have singing and dancing cowboys. (I made sure of that.) "The corn may have been as high as an elephant's eye" in *Oklahoma,* but not in Brooklyn. We had had a lot of success and fun with skits and talent shows that we had performed during the summer months at Camp Variety. I wanted to do a program that would bring some of these kids back during the fall and winter months. Our summer camp program had sort of a "reverse inclusion" component. Many of the siblings of children with disabilities attended camp with their sibling brother or sister, and that worked out great. Why shouldn't the same concept work in a theater and dance program on Saturday mornings?

I sold the plan to our administration and found a little grant money to get things rolling. I hired Wayne Willinger, a local "struggling" actor who had no experience with children's theater but was glad for the stipend. The concept was to accept any kids who showed up on Saturday whether they had disabilities or not. Wayne would assess their talents on the go and present some "plays" to them for their consideration with the objective of working on their social interaction and acting skills to put together a production that could be presented to family and friends.

People get too wrapped up in how kids from diverse backgrounds will respond to one another and try to set up interactive skits or counsel kids on what it's like to be different. Some differences may require some explanation but for the most part, kids are pretty accepting of one another. Our program had white kids, Black kids, Asian kids and Latino kids, and among them were kids with varying degrees of disabilities. When you put kids in a room with a common objective and treat all of them with respect - and they sense that you really want them to succeed—they succeed.

Differences become unimportant. I remember one day walking into our gym during a break from the theater practice and coming upon this heated argument between David Price, a white teenager who had cerebral palsy and used an electric wheelchair for mobility, and Tyson Sandford-Griffin, a Black teenager with no visible disability, about two NFL Ravens' football players and which of the two was the better player. There was no one else around and they were both going at it. I could not have cared less about the argument, but what struck me was that this was just a normal exchange between two teenage boys, both huge Ravens' fans who were both oblivious to the other's differences.

The plays that were performed by the Variety Children's Theatre and Dance program were always the well-known productions, such as *The Lion King, The Wizard of OZ and Annie.* For more than a decade this program offered life-changing experiences for so many kids. Mary Gardner provided the nurturing, her daughter Robin prepared lunches and served as "sergeant-at-arms" (in a good way), and my daughter Emma (who was not under my direct supervision, so I don't think this was a nepotism issue) was also an integral part of the program in its early years. Emma and the dance instructor Beth Ferrell, who taught dance in addition to having a PhD in physical therapy, did a great job and were positive role models for all of the participants, especially the girls. There was a lot of peer teaching as well. Some of these kids went on to college and I believe their experiences in this program influenced them. I think it was one of the best programs that was offered during my tenure as the Program Coordinator for the Therapeutic Recreation Division.

# WINTER
### (But Early Winter…I Hope)
## 2007-present

## Becoming Orphans

On February 22, 2007, Hazel passed away. My brother Skip and I became orphans. I have already encapsulated Hazel's life, but I can never do it justice. I probably got closer to her after Jack's death and when she started experiencing health problems in her 80's. She loved life. I remember a doctor discussing her heart problems with her at some point during her hospitalization at Washington County Hospital in Hagerstown. He asked her about a procedure that might prolong her life. What did she think about that? Her response was, "Well, I want to live as long as I can."

I think she had a good life. I'm sure she wished she could have achieved more but she really did much more than she may have realized. She was a great friend to so many people, including our neighbors and the people she had worked with at the *Herald Mail* Newspaper Company, and she was a great mother to both Skip and me. She was also a surrogate mother to our "sister" Linda Cronauer. Linda was my childhood friend, Joyce Conrad's niece. Linda and her friend from elementary school used to come through our backyard as a shortcut when they came home from school each day from the time they were in elementary school all the way through high school. Hazel befriended Linda. Over time Linda became a close family friend to Hazel and remained so throughout Hazel's life, so I felt compelled to give her an inclusion in my autobiography. Both Skip and I appreciated Linda's involvement in Hazel's life, especially in Hazel's later years.

Hazel was a creative writer. She had a knack for writing witty poetry, most of which she shared with friends and family. She probably could have published what she had written, but I don't think that possibility occurred to her. Hazel was also an incredible grandmother. She got such a kick out of Kate, Emma and Michael, and they too have great memories of her. I think the greatest legacy that you can leave is that you were loved by your family and friends. Hazel had such a legacy.

## Paris Encore

Part of Hazel and Jack's legacy was the inheritance that they left Skip and me. I really don't think that had been a concern for me, but it really was a nice gift. It certainly made Cass's and my life easier at that time and provided us with some discretionary income for ourselves and our kids. We wanted to do something for Kate, Emma and Michael that would help them remember how good Hazel and Jack were to all of us. In 2008 we planned a family trip to Paris.

From the time Kate and Emma were little, Disney World had been implanted in their minds as a fairy-tale trip. Unexpectedly Michael came along in 1990. We told them when Michael was old enough, we'd consider making that trip, although neither Cass nor I ever really contemplated it. The idea of dragging kids around all day, standing in long lines for rides in the hot sun, eating $6.00 hot dogs, the worse vacation ever—that was what Disney World represented to us. The same experiences could be had at Hershey Park and Busch Gardens with a lot less expense and personal angst.

Cass and I decided that to compensate for our personal half-promises, we would take all of them to Paris with the money bequeathed to us by my parents. Michael had just graduated from high school. Emma had just graduated from college and Kate was just starting her professional career. It was probably the last time we could do something like this as a family. Paris is far and away better than Disney World, regardless of what the television ads say about "Magic Mountain."

We took the kids all over the city. Cass took our daughters shopping (mostly window shopping) to all of the upscale fashion boutiques in the "City of Lights," and I took Michael to all of the skateboard parks I could find in remote parts of Paris. We got there using the Paris Metro, which is an adventurous experience in itself. Of course, we visited the Jardins du Luxembourg, the Eiffel Tower and many of the famous museums. The Louvre was a family trip. As we walked throughout this beautiful museum, I couldn't help but think again to myself, "These works are pretty good." It was a memorable trip, and I was so grateful to Hazel and Jack enabling this wonderful family experience.

## A Big Mistake

From 1989 until 2010 I was the Director of Therapeutic Recreation for the Baltimore City Department of Recreation and Parks. In 2010 there was one of many "changing of the guards" in our Department and Dr. Dwayne Thomas took over our Department as the Actor Director of Recreation and Parks. "Doc" must have seen something in me that made him think I would be a good choice for the job he vacated, Chief of Recreation. He asked me to take this position and I was flattered that he asked me and I accepted. What an incredible mistake on both of our parts.

I remember a friend and colleague of mine, Rebecca Ebaugh, an administrative assistant, warning about the psychological effect that my predecessors experienced as Chiefs of Recreation. I of course ignored her warnings, thinking that I was the one person who could make a positive difference in the thirty-some recreation centers in the different communities throughout the city. I should have listened to my colleague. I learned that politics overruled my idealism. Doc Thomas was a visionary and may have been an outstanding Director of Recreation and Parks but he too succumbed to politics. Doc was relieved of his duties at the end of 2010 and I was relieved that I could retire.

Despite the trauma that I experienced in my last year, as I reflect on my career with the Baltimore City Department of Recreation and

Parks, I am proud of what I accomplished and the great relationships that I developed with so many incredible and talented people. It was a wonderful experience, and I will be forever grateful to Ralph Jones, Jr., for bringing me on board in 1989 and providing me with my career.

## Whoops, I Did It Again

About a month after I retired from the city, representatives from Special Olympics Maryland approached me about taking over the Baltimore area Special Olympics program. They were actually recruiting me and again I made the same mistake that I made the year before with Recreation and Parks in Baltimore City.

They felt I was the one who could turn around a program in the city that had been faltering for years and for some inexplicable reason, I thought maybe I could. I thought wrong.

I spent nine months spinning my wheels that concluded with arguably one of the worst Baltimore City Special Olympic Games in the Spring of 2012. Having said that, I did enjoy the staff and athletes that I met during this time. There were simply challenges related to both Special Olympics and the Baltimore City school system that were beyond my ability to correct. I should have learned from my mistakes. It's pretty apparent that I'm a slow learner.

I did have some good experiences during my time at Special Olympics. For about one month during the winter months, kids were bused to a Baltimore City Recreation and Parks ice-skating rink in North Baltimore for skating instruction in preparation for a final competition, which included both figure skating, a skill component for kids who were more physically and mentally disabled, and a racing competition. All of the kids received rented figure skates that had seen their best days decades before. Regardless of the competitive event, you wore figure skates.

One of the athletes, Annu, was entered in competitive speed skating, and his speed skates were a well-worn pair of size 13 beige figure skates. Annu is my all-time favorite Special Olympics athlete. I guess he's now in his early 30's. Back then he was a tall, skinny 18- or 19-year-old Black kid from an extremely poor area of Baltimore City. Annu was and is a very good athlete as well as being an excellent spokesperson for Special Olympics and I think he competes in every sport that is offered by Special Olympics. He may have had some intellectual challenges but whatever they were, he always seemed to overcome them. He's another one of those people that I have met in my life who is a survivor. He loves Special Olympics. If there was some kind of competition going on in any part of the city in the evening or weekends, and if Annu had to walk ten miles to get there, he'd walk the ten miles to the program in the dead of winter and walk home if no one offered him a ride. Annu's greatest wish was that he could be a professional athlete representing Special Olympics. I hope his wish comes true. Back to speed skating.

One of the last ice-skating events is held at the North Baltimore arena each January is a speed skating contest where more accomplished skaters speed skate around a pre-determined distance on the ice rink. I think that the race Annu was scheduled to be in was four times around the rink. St. Elizabeth's School is a private school for kids with disabilities in northeast Baltimore. It is a great school and they are able to provide their students with better services than public schools in the city. They had a speed skater who had actual speed skates, and he knew how to skate. After watching the city kids pretty much stumble, fall, get up and resume their race, it was a pleasure to see this young man smoothly skate around the rink with ease and confidence.

Annu was in the same race as this St. E's skater. He had his trusty, beat-up figure skates laced and he was ready. I had never seen Annu on skates before and had no idea what to expect. The gun went off for the race, and the St. E's skater was off and was in good form. He immediately shot out to a lead. I watched Annu and immediately noticed that he had a different skating technique. He was running on the ice in his skates—no, he was galloping on the ice. I had never seen anything like it. When the skaters were about to complete the fourth and final lap, the kid from St. E's was about a half an oval's distance ahead of second place Annu. The rest of the skaters may have been two laps behind. As I watched Annu, his gallop on the ice began to increase and he started to gain on the St. E's skater. The next thing I knew, Annu was galloping at a pace I can't imagine any skater had ever galloped before. He caught up to the St. E's skater on the last curve, and with a burst of speed never before seen in the history of speed skating, he overcame the St. E's skater at the finish line and won a gold medal.

I do not think anyone else in the building had watched and appreciated this race the way I did. When I told this story back at the Special Olympics headquarters the next day, everyone was incredulous. They were laughing so hard at my recollection of what had transpired the previous day on ice. No one else could ever duplicate the race that Annu had "galloped." If he would have been on my ice hockey team way back when I was a kid on the Conococheague Creek in Williamsport, Maryland, along with my uncle who could only skate backwards, we really would have changed the game of ice hockey forever.

## Prioritizing My Priorities

The previous two years took a physical and psychological toll on me. I still have nightmares about these career-ending work experiences. I was pushing 230 lbs. and started taking blood pressure medicine. I was becoming a power forward when I had always considered myself to be a feathery, finesse-playing shooting guard who had the ability to average 4 points a game consistently regardless of the level of competition. It was time to start making a comeback; but before I did, Cass and I took our fourth trip to Paris in 2012.

It was not a planned trip until the year before it occurred. Cass found out that the International Alzheimer's Association's conference was to be held in Paris in 2012. Her organization covered her costs. My expenditures included the cost of an airline ticket, and thankfully Cass agreed to share her hotel room, so this became an unexpected and greatly appreciated opportunity. During the day, while Cass learned of the many new developments in the quest for a cure for Alzheimer's Disease, I wandered the streets of Paris. We would meet on breaks, and there were numerous opportunities for us to do things together during the day and in the evenings. When Cass did have to work, however, I always told her what a great job she was doing before I wandered off to a bistro for a glass of wine, a petit beignet and some cheese. I mean, I had to occupy my time.

I also took a brand-new deflated basketball with me to Paris on this trip. It was not my intention to try out for a French professional team (although the thought did cross my mind). I had two reasons for packing the basketball. The first was to shoot hoops on the basketball court located in Les Jardins du Luxembourg. It's not like there is a court full of hoopsters playing ball on this court; in fact, hardly anyone plays there, and I'm sure that the reasons are because the basketball standards are rather antiquated, and the times that I have been there the rims which are probably a bit higher than they should be, do not have nets, which to me is almost sacrilegious, but I'm in France. Maybe the netting is needed for fishing or macrame. I attracted the attention of a few people, all of whom were curious about seeing a 65-year-old man running around by himself shooting baskets in a park whose primary raison d'être is its historical beauty.

The other reason that I brought the ball was to go to a local outdoor court and maybe get into a pick-up game with some joueurs francais (French players). Down the street from where we stayed was an old and barely used court. (There are some great French basketball players, but soccer is still the sport of choice.) I started shooting, and eventually I attracted the attention of some young teenagers who looked to be of Algerian descent, and I invited them to play. I could immediately tell that soccer was their game, but they seemed to enjoy my attention. When we finished, I created a shooting contest where the winner of the contest could keep the ball. Soccer aside, basketball became much more of a competitive endeavor for these players at that point. Their shooting skills improved dramatically with a free basketball on the line. A winner eventually emerged after many desperate shots from all angles of the court. I presented the winner with the ball, a pump and a needle. It was sort of an Olympic moment if you will. I then left the park and walked back up the street with a smile on my face, knowing that I had accomplished my international basketball mission. The world would be a better place because of my humanitarian efforts.

One of the special trips that Cass and I were able to take together was a train trip to the small city of Chartres in southwest France. The Chartres Cathedrale was built between 1193 and 1250. We also visited the Musee des Beaux-Arts, a fine arts museum adjacent to the cathedral, and I'd have to say, the art works there were pretty good. This was our fourth trip to Paris. We hope to go there again in 2022 for our 50th wedding anniversary. On verra…

## Beating Age

When we returned from Paris, I was fully retired. It was then that I began my personal rehab work to lose weight and reestablish some normalcy in my life. I joined a local gym here in Mt. Airy and began my training in earnest. Also, I started playing stand-up basketball again at a recreation center in Howard County, Maryland with a bunch of aging athletes like myself. This program ran three days a week, and I'd spend about two or three hours on each of these days hobbling (but a silky-smooth hobble) up and down a basketball court, thinking in my mind that I still had it (always a legend in my own mind). Playing with these guys has been a blast, but even I find myself laughing at some of the players as they too envision themselves as young players fluidly moving around when the majority of them struggle to get from one part of the court to the other. Who would have thought that basketball was one of those lifetime sports? I guess I did.

## No Laughing Matter

In 2015 I fell out of a tree. I don't know why, but I can't help thinking that whoever is reading this is chuckling when they read this (and saying to themselves, "Serves you right for writing this book.") There was a huge tree in my neighbor's yard that had been struck by lightning a year or so prior to the story I'm about to tell. There were dead branches hanging over into our yard. Now, our neighbor appears to be a bit eccentric. I won't elaborate other than to say that he doesn't cut his grass or take care of anything related to the grounds on which his house sits. I guess that's his prerogative, but it makes for some communication problems. At any rate, I decided that he wasn't going to take this tree down, but I was certainly entitled to remove the dead limbs from his tree that were hanging in our yard. I got a ladder and an electric saw, climbed up into the tree and started cutting limbs. I was about ready to come down, but then I saw one limb that I thought I might be able to reach out and eliminate. When I reached for it, I knew immediately that I was going to fall. I prepared for impact. I fell from 12', a drop that I learned later kills 80% of those falling from that height.

Fortunately, I threw the saw as I was falling. Instinctively I changed my position in mid-air so I wouldn't fall on my artificial hip. I landed with a sort of thud-like bounce. My first reaction was to gauge if I was still alive, and to my surprise, I was. Next, could I get up? No, I could not. I started moving other body parts and realized two things: 1) I did some damage to my shoulder, and 2) I broke the tibia and fibula in my right leg. Fortunately, my son Michael was at home. He called an ambulance, and I was off to Shock Trauma in Baltimore for a two-day stay, operation included, and then I was sent to a rehabilitation center for about a week. Cass was not too thrilled with me. I tried to explain that I was cutting the limbs out of the tree for her, but she maintained that I had no business being up in a tree in the first place. She may have had a point but I was hoping for a little bit of compassion.

When I landed on the ground, I immediately assessed that it would take me six months to get back on the basketball court. What could be more important than that for a 68-year-old man? When I finally got home, I did a little in-home rehab for a couple of weeks and then I started back to the gym. I had a walking boot on, so my first exercise was swimming, and that worked out well. Changing in and out of my swimsuit was more of a workout than swimming, but once in the water I could swim laps as well as walk gingerly in the swim lanes.

The other thing I did was ride on an Expresso stationary bike. I rode with my boot on (this boot was not made for walking), but there was no real pressure on my leg, and it was a way to get a cardio workout. The bike that I rode kept tabs on everything. I could count my miles, how many calories I burned, how fast I went, etc., and I could ride about a dozen different routes from hilly to flat. I chose flat. I soon realized that the type of bike that I was riding was used all over the world, and I could compare my stats with people from France, for example. It became an obsession. I use my phone and ear pods to listen to youtube music, and would ride my bike for a couple of hours at a time.

Soon I was one of the top riders in the world—on a stationary bike—which is a very dubious achievement to say the least. I decided I would go around the world on my bike. The circumference of the earth is 24,901 miles, and I figured conservatively that I could ride around the earth in about six years, assuming I had good weather, and that was my goal. As it turned out, my bike riding became an obsessive-compulsive exercise, and the first year I racked up about 8,000 miles. Towards the middle of 2017 I was close to completing my world tour. I asked Cass if she thought the Alzheimer's Association would consider my turning this into a fundraiser for the organization. They accepted my idea, and I started soliciting money on Facebook and through family and friends. My goal was to raise $7,500.

On June 21, 2017, the television cameras were in the gym as I rode my last mile. I reached my goal, and it was a fun way to assist the organization. I got newspaper coverage and a nice plaque for my efforts. When asked, "What's next?" my response was, "Ride around again, but this time I would take more time to meet people from different parts of the world and learn more about their cultures."

On my second ride around the earth, I crossed the finish line at Health Unlimited in Mt. Airy, Maryland, at 11:00 a.m. on August 19, 2021. In total for the six-year, twice-around-the-world and change tour, I have raised a total of a little over $10,000 for Alzheimer's research. I believe, if my math is correct, that comes out to about $.20 a mile. I know that some of you may require a visual as proof, so follow this link:

https://www.localdmv.com/news/maryland/50000-a-mount-airy-man-bikes-to-raise-funds-to-battle-alzheimers-disease/

Coincidentally, the media outlet that covered my final moments as I crossed the line was *The Herald Mail* newspaper from Hagerstown, Maryland, the same paper that covered my grand slam for Culler's Esso Little League team 62 years ago. I've come full circle in more ways than one; actually, two.

When I sent this link to family and friends, Rochelle Lessner, a friend from our Peace Corps group, suggested that stationary bike riding should be included in the Olympics and then went one step further to say that there should be "synchronized" stationary bike riding. I think it's an excellent idea, and after finishing this book, I'm going to draft a letter to the International Olympic Committee and demand that the new sport be included in the Olympics in Paris in 2024. Cass and I will participate in mixed doubles. I am thinking about our choreography as I write. We will definitely be wearing red, white and blue sequin-embellished leotards. I, of course, will shave my legs to lesson wind resistance.

## COVID SCHMOVID

The years between 2017 and COVID-19 in 2021 were uneventful (with the exception of my riding around the world for a second time on a stationary bike of course) but the COVID-19 virus changed the world in an eventful but unfortunate way. In my lifetime I have never experienced anything like this. I had to stop my second tour of the earth on my stationary bike because my gym was closed. I most certainly would've completed my 50,000-mile objective in 2020 if not for being inconvenienced by COVID-19. I was in Western Australia (I imagined) when I received word to come home; from Perth to this side of the earth.

Like all families, our family experienced difficulties that challenged us, but we were able to weather the storm and were very fortunate not to have had to endure the terrible hardships that many families have experienced. Our daughter Emma, son-in-law Brian and our grand-kids, Hazel, Mark and Ruth moved in with Cass, me and our son Michael. Emma and Brian and after they sold their house in Frederick, Maryland, during the spring of 2020. Selling their home before buying a new one coincided with the onset of COVID-19. Many people were stranded in their homes and remained isolated from their family and friends for over a year. We were isolated together, so we conveniently co-existed during those difficult times. Our other daughter Kate and her husband Marshall live in Baltimore City and were stuck in their house throughout the pandemic, but we managed a few "co-vert" visits, and "Zoom" became a commonly-used word in our vocabulary. COVID-19 has been more than a "Where were you when this happened?" kind of thing.

Our family was fortunate to survive the pandemic in pretty good shape, but so many families have suffered losses as a result of this unforeseen pandemic. It has been an incredibly sad time. Despite political upheaval and controversies, Americans are resilient. I am confident that we will begin to get back to some sense of normalcy in the near future.

## Obits

During the past couple of years, a little before COVID-19 and during the epidemic, some dear friends and family members have passed on. These people played a special part in my life and I wanted to acknowledge them for their contributions to my life.

**Rich Melby** – Rich was friend from the time I was in grade school until he died in 2019 from esophageal cancer. He was the one person from Hagerstown that I maintained a relationship with throughout my life. Rich was a craftsman. He created beautiful furniture, furniture that can be more accurately described as art. He laughed with me and gave me encouragement when I needed it. I did not see him often but when I did, it was a comfortable and memorable time.

**Brian Kern** – Brian was a Peace Corps Volunteer with Cass and I in Maradi, Niger from 1979 to 1981. He was from upstate New York. Brian was a little wiry guy who was very smart and very fearless. He worked in a agricultural program in the Peace Corps and he certainly did what he could to the best of his abilities. His real claim to fame though was his total immersion into the Nigerien culture. He was fluent in both Hausa and Zarma, two traditional Nigerien languages. There were many Nigerien women who were taken by his language skills and charm. Brian passed away in 2020 from a rare type of cancer. Brian wrote several books about his life experiences during and after the Peace Corps. He lived his life to the fullest.

**Frank (Buddy) Knapp III** – Frank, who was from Hagerstown also, was one of my roommates at the University of Baltimore. He was always such a positive person. He loved life. He died after a lengthy battle with esophageal cancer at age 74. Buddy was always a good friend who laughed at my jokes. Those who knew him during our days at the University of Baltimore will always remember him fondly.

**John Bruce Baker** – Bruce was my brother-in-law. I mentioned Bruce earlier in the book. He was a Presbyterian minister. Bruce is the person who managed to solicit help from his community for basketball shoes for my basketball team in Maradi, Niger in 1981 when Cass and I were in the Peace Corps. Besides taking on the ministerial role of marrying my daughters, my nieces and nephews and being the minister for Hazel's funeral when she passed in 2007, he was a minister, counselor, mentor and friend to countless numbers of people in the many places that he and Julie lived over the years. Bruce died in 2021 from an undiagnosed neurological illness. The illness was terribly debilitating but through it all he maintained a remarkable dignity and made the best of his life during this time. Bruce practiced what he preached. That is all that can be asked of anyone who sees the good in all people. He was a good man.

**Jan Douglas** – Jan was my friend, Tom Stough's wife. Jan died in 2021 from pancreatic cancer. Jan was a dear friend of both my wife, Cass and me for over fifty years. Jan was a retired social worker from Baltimore City. She was incredibly smart, funny and amazingly insightful. She was loved by her family, friends, staff and clients, and positively affected the lives of all those she touched over the years. Jan was a joy to be around and have as a friend. She is deeply missed.

**Christopher Paul Walker** – On January 5, 2022, my brother-in-law Chris, Cass's second youngest brother, died of pancreatic cancer. Chris was preceded in death by his older brother, Bernie who also died of pancreatic cancer in 2015. Chris, a talented cabinet-maker, is remembered for his ability to find joy and meaning in life through his skills with plants, creative arts, dogs and close family and friends.

**Stephen (Steve) and Djeswende (Wendy) Reid** – On Thursday, April 21, 2022 the bodies of our dear friends Steve and Wendy Reid were discovered on a hiking trail near their home in Concord, New Hampshire. They were murdered by an unknown assailant for an as yet unknown reason. Steve was a Peace Corps volunteer with Cass and me in Niger, West Africa from 1979 until 1981. He was an All-American young man who graduated from Notre Dame University and joined the Peace Corps to make a difference in the lives of people in a third-world country. As an English teacher Steve provided young Nigerians with a language skill that would be beneficial to them in their future. He immersed himself in the Nigerian culture, learning not only French but additionally he became fluent in the Hausa language, the main local language of Niger. When he finished his Peace Corps tour and returned to the United States, he met Wendy, a young woman from Togo who was teaching physical education in Washington, D.C. Steve's experiences in Africa must have drawn Wendy, a fluent French speaker to him. They just clicked. They both went on to careers with the Peace Corps and U.S.A.I.D. in Africa as well as in other countries suffering from catastrophic events. They offered significant emergency relief to people world-wide who were undergoing terrible hardships. They were the nicest people one could imagine. They will be deeply missed by their children, their family and many, many friends.

# Adieu

Life has a way of introducing you to so many interesting people and situations. I like to make mental notes of things that have occurred in my life and I find great pride and joy in reflecting back on the people I have known and the wonderful experiences that have come my way. I want to thank my wife, Cass for her love and support over so many years. June 17, 2022 will mark our 50th wedding anniversary. I also want to thank my children, Kate, Emma and Michael for joy and pride they have given us. All of them are remarkably successful and kind, caring people. They have graduated from college and have chosen careers which help others to have a better quality of life. I think Cass most certainly was their biggest influence but I hope that I have contributed to their success in some small way. I hope that my grandchildren, Hazel, Mark and Ruth inherit the kindness and intelligence of their parents and the ingenuity, empathy and wisdom of their grandmother, Cass. All of them like to laugh so my contribution will have to be the "humor gene," which is no laughing matter.

Thank you for taking the time to wade through this rambling saga of my life (especially to my copy editor, who immediately knew when she took this editing job on that she had made a big mistake.) If it is any consolation, I am relatively certain that this will be my first and last effort at writing a book.

I doubt my life's story will achieve any critical acclaim. There might be a Pulitzer in the offing but only if "writing randomly" becomes a literary style. If that should happen, I could see some well-known critic exclaiming, "This guy can really ramble!"

As a parting gesture of appreciation, I am concluding with a poem for all of you. I think William Butler Yeats would agree with the message that this poem conveys.

## Obits and Pieces – Michael Jon Naugle

Now you have struggled through this story,
The pieces of my life,
From Halfway to the very end,
The years also with my wife.
Some stories go on and on,
They seem so arbitrary;
If written well this could have been,
A half-page obituary.

## Le Fin